Counseling for Church Leaders

COUNSELING FOR CHURCH LEADERS

John W. Drakeford

BROADMAN PRESS ● Nashville, Tennessee

© 1961 • BROADMAN PRESS
Nashville, Tennessee

Second Printing

422-110

Library of Congress catalog card number: 61-12412

Printed in the United States of America
1.AL6513

Preface

THIS BOOK seeks, above everything else, to be practical. It comes from the practical experience of the author as pastor, chaplain, youth worker, professor, and director of a counseling center. The simple thesis is that many people needing counseling turn very naturally to the church. In this setting the already overworked pastor cannot possibly cope with all the demands upon him. The answer set forth here is that the layman must be increasingly utilized, and suggestions are made to help in preparing him for the task.

A great musical masterpiece has a recurring theme or motif. While this book is no work of art, it, too, has a motif—the therapeutic effect of a sympathetic listener. This motif first appears in chapter 1, which shows that great biblical figures used listening as a vital part of their work in leadership. The motif reappears in chapter 3 in the discussion of the work of the layman and is expanded at considerable length in chapters 4 and 5, which consider the need for the art of listening. Later, gaining rapport is seen to have a relationship to listening; and in the exposition of "the heart of the counseling process," the theme comes to its crescendo with a more technical, yet practical, exposition of the concept. In a minor manner the motif is repeated in the discussion of insight; and, later, listening is seen as important in working with the sick, helping in marriage problems, and the effective functioning of women counselors.

The book is in three parts. The first part discusses the normal relationships within the church, introducing the layman to personality concepts which he can use. In the second part the counseling process is followed through its movement from beginning to conclusion, and the third part deals with specialized considerations in counseling.

Contents

Part One

Understanding and Helping People in the Church

THE CHRISTIAN church has a ministry to individuals, and the layman working within the framework of a church organization must, above everything else, understand people. The entire setup of a modern church—its buildings, nurseries, classrooms, visual aids, musical instruments, and professional staff—exists for the primary purpose of helping people. In the first section of this book attention is focused upon the layman's responsibility in normal church relationships.

Historically, Christians have looked to the Bible for their inspiration. For this reason the first chapter focuses upon the Bible's message concerning the interpersonal relationships of life. A different approach to the study of the Bible is made in an effort to show the ministry of counseling found there. Laymen loom large in the biblical counseling ministry.

Without realizing its full significance, we have accepted the statement that man is fearfully and wonderfully made. Chapter 2 deals with man and makes a brief examination of his personality. Significant concepts such as the unconscious, adjustment mechanisms, and unruly emotions are considered.

The distinctive and special ministry of the layman becomes the focus of attention in chapter 3. The meaning of the term "vocation" and the enlightening discoveries of marriage counseling leaders in England are examined. The special and distinctive ministries of the layman in his informal contacts and organizational relationships are shown to reveal special possibilities for his ministry.

The importance of listening, already noted in the chapter on the Bible, is now given a more extended treatment. Chapter 4, in a popular way, treats the dynamics of personality by showing what listening does for people. From this, chapter 5 leads to a discussion of "the art of listening," leaving the layman with the most significant tool for the exercise of his special ministry.

1. Counseling in the Bible

THE WORD counseling has come to a position of prominence in our vocabularies. It is a popular "conversation piece" and people speak with easy familiarity of inferiority complexes, nervous breakdowns, hypnosis, and the analyst's couch. Some see this as an expression of our age of anxiety, while others look upon the whole thing as merely a modern fad that will go the same way as bustles, pole sitting, goldfish swallowing, and twirling hula hoops. A church deacon chided his pastor about his counseling activities and said, "When I was a young man, we didn't have anybody to counsel us and we got by all right." However, an examination of church history shows that long before it developed into a formalized concept, counseling was carried on within churches. Even earlier than this we find that the pages of the Bible have within them many instances of counseling.

Some people feel that the Bible is only concerned with man's salvation and has nothing to say about his personality and its development. Zilboorg and Henry's monumental writing *A History of Medical Psychology* quotes, with approval, the words of George Sydney Bett: "The scriptures present only one side of human life, that which concerns the idea of salvation; for the rest the treatment of man is incidental." [1] Nothing could be further from the truth. It is true that the Bible is not a textbook of psychotherapy or a counselor's case book. It is a history of a nation and a developing religion. Nevertheless, it has much to say about individuals and is very vocal on the subject of interpersonal relationships.

3

Holding Up Moses' Arms

The graphic picture of Aaron and Hur holding up Moses' arms during the battle of the Israelites against the forces of Amalek was a picture of the assistance which the great leader needed. Another instance is found when Moses' father-in-law Jethro noticed that Moses sat all day long listening to the complaints of the people and "judging" them. Jethro suggested an arrangement so that others could assist Moses by sharing the counseling load.

The plan of organization is expressed in Jethro's exhortation: "Appoint them to supervise groups of thousands, of hundreds, of fifties, and of tens" (Ex. 18:21, Moffatt). Bishop Ellicott, in his commentary, says: "An organization of the entire people on a decimal system is implied in the arrangement suggested." [2] Dr. R. Othal Feather of Southwestern Baptist Theological Seminary School of Religious Education has shown the similarity between this primitive organization and the organizational pattern used in some of our larger Sunday schools. The Sunday school itself is represented by the division of one thousand. Then, come the divisions of hundreds, which are the age groups, such as Adult, Young People, Intermediate, Junior, Primary, and Beginner. Within these age groupings are the divisions of fifty, representing the departments, as with the Adult group where there would be Adult I, Adult II, Adult III, and so on. The fifties have divisions of ten, representing the classes. The plan of Jethro sounds strangely modern in a day when emphasis is laid upon small class groups for both teaching and discussion.

Moral qualifications were stressed in the selection of Moses' assistants, "Moreover thou shalt provide out of all the people able men, such as fear God, men of truth, hating covetousness" (Ex. 18:21). There were three qualifications for these counselors. They were to be able, religious, and honest. These qualifications would be a good starting point for anyone who plans to help others within a religious setting.

Availability is used to describe the freedom of access which the counselors have to the counselor. Availability is seen to be significant here, "And let them judge the people at all seasons" (Ex.

18:22). It will be seen later that availability is a vital factor in the relationship of a religious worker with small groups and that the church leader's availability is one of the most useful aspects of his ministry.

Referral is a term used to describe the process by which a person is placed in contact with help beyond the counselor's capacity to give, and in this setting is seen a primitive, yet effective, referral system. One man in ten would be capable of counseling in small matters, but his counselees might be dissatisfied and the matter could then be referred to the ruler of fifty. If there were still a feeling of dissatisfaction, it could be referred, in turn, to the ruler of one hundred and then the ruler of one thousand. Finally, if the situation were really complex, it could be taken to Moses himself.

As primitive as the setting was, certain elements vital to the counseling process were present. Organization, an emphasis on moral qualifications, and a referral system all played a part in these early efforts.

Street Counseling

The modern counselor's office with its waiting room, subdued lighting, and couch is often seen as necessary for successful counseling. It was not so with the wise men of biblical times. They gathered at the gate, the busiest place in town, and carried on a counseling relationship. Jacobus, in *A Standard Bible Dictionary*, makes reference to Jeremiah 18:18. "For the law shall not perish from the priest nor counsel from the wise nor the word from the prophet." [3] He concludes that the intellectual classes of ancient Israel were spoken of as priests, prophets, and the wise. The function of the priest was to give instruction; the prophet to give the word; and the wise to give the counsel. The wise men performed the functions of teachers and counselors, with these two roles overlapping and intermingling. Significantly enough, to this day in many ways counseling is best seen as an educational procedure.

The wisdom literature has many references indicating the type of problems the wise men discussed with their counselees.

Obviously, *personal virtues* were mentioned, "He that ruleth his spirit [is better] than he that taketh a city" (Prov. 16:32). The businessman of that day apparently talked with the wise man about his problems, and an insight into some of the transactions of the market place is given by the statement "It is naught, it is naught, saith the buyer: but when he is gone his way, then he boasteth " (Prov. 20:14). Family counseling was also involved; hence, the statement "It is better to dwell in a corner of the house top, than with a brawling woman in a wide house" (Prov. 21:9).

The wise men, in the open air, amid the dirt, dust, and distractions of an Oriental city gate, were able nevertheless to give individual counsel to those in need. A re-examination of the ministry of these wise men may serve to encourage today's harassed church teacher in his counseling ministry.

• *Counselors of Job*

The book of Job comes to grips with the problem of suffering. Rabbi Gerber in his book *The Psychology of the Suffering Mind* seeks to elucidate the psychological issues in the experience of Job. Gerber concludes that Job's illness was probably psychological and quotes Dunbar and Slaughter as stating that Job's skin trouble was psychosomatic. The skin feels all the sensations and serves as the individual's means of expression and relationship with the outside world. Recognition of this has come in popular expressions—"the blushing bride," "paling with anger," and "flushing with resentment." Gerber finally concludes that Job's trouble was involutional melancholia, which he defines as the depressions of middle and later life.

Job's friends tried to help him, and some of the counseling techniques of that day are to be seen in their efforts. Job's wife advised a very simple method—suicide. All of Job's friends utilized *silence:* "For seven days and seven nights they sat beside him on the ground; none said a word to him" (Job 2:13, Moffatt). Gerber says this has given rise to a Jewish custom that in the case of bereavement, the comforter should never be the first to speak. The second technique of Job's friends was not as good as the first. It was *intellectual interpretation,* which involved trying to persuade him by appealing to his intellect and reason and to show him the cause of his trouble. Unfortunately, Job did not see the situation the way his friends did, and they revealed their inability to be good counselors by reacting vehemently and turning the counseling session into a debate.

Gerber concludes that the main value from the experience was the opportunity for Job to express himself. By giving vent to his emotions, he was able to ultimately work through his melancholia.

The Pastor of Sheep and Men

David is known as the shepherd boy. It seems that from his earliest days he developed a particular ability to help people. When King Saul was emotionally distraught and needed help in his emotional problems, his servants spoke to him of David's reputation. Thus David was brought to the palace. In counseling terminology it would be said that David established rapport with Saul as he gained the disturbed king's confidence—it has been suggested that Saul was suffering from depressions which were both suicidal and homocidal. As David played the harp, he showed the power of music to relieve the king's dementia. Once again, in modern terminology it would be said that David used an elementary form of music therapy, which calmed Saul and enabled him to cope with his depression. Later, when David was in danger from Achish, the king of Gath, and endeavored to escape, he pretended to be mad.

And he changed his behavior before them, and feigned himself mad in their hands, and scrabbled on the doors of the gate, and let his spittle fall down upon his beard. Then said Achish unto his servants, Lo, ye see the man is mad: wherefore then have ye brought him to me? (1 Sam. 21:13-14).

From this display, it is obvious that David was familiar with the symptoms of psychoses and had probably observed psychotic people very closely.

A counseling relationship is very delicate and may take many twists and turns. The counselee often comes to feel very strongly toward his counselor, and this emotional bond is called transference. A *negative transference* is the expression used to describe the process by which feelings of hostility which the counselee has toward something else are felt toward the counselor.

Saul had a negative transference as the relationship with David developed and at times even tried to murder David. Throughout this vacillation of affection, David continued to accept Saul. He was *nonjudgmental;* and after Saul had made three attempts to his life, he still spared him when he could have retaliated. One counseling authority speaks of the "expectation of nonretaliation," meaning that every counselee has the right to feel that he can reveal confidences to the counselor without fear of a violation of trust. The lesson dramatized here is that the counselor must never in any way "strike back" at his counselee.

Although he did not always manage his personal life in the most mature way, David evidenced an unusual ability to get close to people in order to help them. By his acceptance and skilful handling of Saul's activity, he exemplified aspects of counseling important to the skilful practitioner of the art.

Prophets, Priests, Kings, and Shepherds

The prophet was a "forthteller;" consequently, many of the statements of the prophetic writings are from this frame of reference. They are of more help in the concept of preaching than in the idea of counseling. There are, however, indications of other techniques. In Malachi there was a glimmering of what psychologists would now call group therapy, "Then they that feared the Lord spake often one to another (Mal. 3:16). Group fellowship of godly people has often given therapeutic support to needy members of a group.

In discussing the shepherds of Israel, Ezekiel, strangely enough, speaks of the temporal leader as the shepherd. In all Semitic languages, according to Rossell, the word "king" comes from the root word "counselor." Ezekiel rebukes the shepherds and discusses the qualifications of a shepherd in a negative way. Stated positively, the shepherd's duties include: strengthening the weak, healing the sick, bandaging up the cripples, recovering those who are driven away, and looking for those who are lost.

Here, again, is seen the difficulty in discovering a well developed ministry of counseling in the Old Testament. Whereas David the shepherd boy was the outstanding figure, the secular ruler now becomes the pastor, responsible for the flock of God.

Jesus, the Counselor

Many activities characteristic of the ministry of Jesus are utilized today in counseling procedures. Jesus knew by insight the condition of man. In John's Gospel it is stated that he "needed not that any should testify of man: for he knew what was in man" (John 2:25). The next verse goes on to say "There was a man of the Pharisees, named Nicodemus" (John 3:1). The verse proceeds to describe aspects of this man's personal life in great detail.

Jesus is generally thought of as the preacher proclaiming a message. He was also the teacher who spent much time instructing his disciples. But Jesus was also a *listener*. On a number of occasions he listened when he might have been expected to speak. A certain lawyer stood up and asked Jesus, "Master, what shall I do to inherit eternal life?" (Luke 10:25). The modern preacher perhaps would have presented his pet formula to such a query; however, Jesus did not. He simply replied, "What is written in the law? how readest thou? (Luke 10:26). The man then gave an explanation of his interpretation of the law while Jesus listened.

Jesus had much to say about listening. Reference to a concordance shows that over two hundred times Jesus exhorted people to hear and to listen. In such statements as "He that hath ears to hear, let him hear" (Mark 4:9), Jesus stressed the importance of listening. He showed his consciousness of the reluctance of men and women to listen as he said "having ears, hear ye not?" (Mark 8:18).

The word "acceptance," as used in counseling, recognizes the worth of the individual without approval of his behavior or implying personal affection. Acceptance was a keynote of the ministry of Jesus. Though he could thunder at the Pharisees and the hypocrites and denounce the religious leaders of his day, when it came to talking to individuals, his ministry took on a very warm and gentle note. In his encounter with the woman at the well, Jesus saw a lonely, sinful person and began a conversation with her. In breaking down her defenses, he got her to the place where she was willing to open her heart and speak freely. The woman taken in adultery was brought before Jesus by the legalistic religious leaders who were prepared to condemn her, but were convicted by their own conscience at Jesus' seering statement, "He that is without sin among you, let him first cast a stone" (John 8:7). Jesus saw beyond the outward facade and understood that, above everything else, this woman wanted to be accepted. He understood, too, that it may have been this very element of not being accepted which led her into her humiliating situation.

Freud's formulations of the importance of slips of the tongue for showing the true content of the unconscious were considered revolutionary and sensational. However, Jesus spoke of the motives coming out of the "heart" of man as showing his inner life. He also said, "Every idle word that men shall speak, they shall give account thereof in the day of judgment" (Matt. 12:36). The implication is that the idle word revealed the real man and was significant nineteen hundred years before Freud formulated his theories.

Jesus was certainly not a psychologist as we think of psychologists today. However, in his understanding of people, his willingness to listen, and his ability to relate himself to others, he used methods similar to those of the modern counselor.

Counseling in the Early Church

The story of the Acts of the Apostles is of the spread of the missionary message across the world. It is primarily a ministry of preaching and proclaiming, but there are glimpses of a ministry akin to counseling. Laymen were appointed to determine the needs of the people and insofar as possible to administer relief. In many ways, their work resembled that of the social worker of our day.

The most outstanding figure in the book of Acts is Paul, whom we think of as a preacher and a theologian; but there were other important aspects of his ministry. A vivid insight into the more personal areas of Paul's work is seen in his address to the Ephesian elders at Miletus. His empathy or capacity to feel for people is indicated in this farewell. English and English illustrate the distinction between empathy and sympathy by saying that the parent may empathize with the child's rage, feeling either pity or amusement, whereas, in sympathy he would rage along with the child. In this attitude of empathy is the implicit idea "I see how you feel."

As Paul tells of shedding many a tear and experiencing many a trial, his words find a strange echo within the heart of the modern church worker. He also alludes to teaching from house to house, and at least one commentator says that "this possibly includes personal and individual counseling." [4]

In the last chapter of Acts is the picture of Paul confined to his home with visitors constantly coming and going. Primarily, these visitors came to consult about matters of church life and belief, but elements of counseling must have entered into the situation. The picture of Paul's talking with his Roman guards; patiently reassuring Onesimus, the runaway slave; commending the daring Epaphroditus, who risked his life to bring the Philippian gift; and counseling with the Jews suggests the breadth of the man who takes the world into his heart, and yet has time to talk with individuals.

Illuminating Letters

The Epistles are generally looked upon as embodying the doctrinal development of the teachings of the early church. In addition to the strong doctrinal emphases and the theological concepts and ideas involved, Paul's epistles to the Romans and the Colossians probably mention more individuals than any other letters of the New Testament. Paul had not visited either of the churches, and the implication is that he took much time to get to know people personally and kept up with where they were and what was happening to them.

In the second epistle to the Corinthians, in the midst of an exposition on the importance of the ministry, Paul inserts a moving biographical statement concerning his "thorn in the flesh." Just what this thorn was has bothered Bible scholars for a long time. Many have agreed that in all probability it was some Eastern disease affecting his eyes, causing him to feel miserable and to look unsightly. Paul tells of seeking deliverance and of God's threefold answer: "My grace is sufficient for thee" (2 Cor. 12:9). In effect, Paul's recital indicated to his readers that there was no easy way of deliverance from life's difficulties. The answer to the problem was in the strengthening of his personality by God's Spirit. The need was not changed circumstances but a changed attitude.

The Galatian letter also has a counseling emphasis. In the midst of his polemic argument against the Judaizers who were detracting from the message of Christ, Paul paused to speak of the shepherding ministry and exhorted the Galatians to be *accepting:* "If a man be overtaken in a fault, ye which are spiritual, restore such an one in the spirit of meekness; considering thyself, lest thou also be tempted" (Gal. 6:1). Later, he indicated the importance of *empathy:* "Bear ye one another's burdens, and so fulfil the law of Christ" (Gal. 6:2). Nevertheless, immediately after emphasizing "feeling into" another person's problem comes a corrective, lest this person should become *dependent.* People are to accept their own responsibilities, "Let every man prove his own work, and then shall he have rejoicing . . . for every man shall bear his own burden" (Gal. 6:4-5).

The pastoral epistles abound with exhortations to those who would minister to others. The bishop is a family man who is to have one wife, to be patient and of good report from without. Deacons are warned not to be "tale-bearers." Then, as now, confidence is a key to the establishment of good counseling relationships.

Summary

The ministry of counseling in the Bible was carried on by many different people. Leaders in the book of Exodus had a ministry very similar to that of Sunday school teachers today. Wise men combined the arts of teaching and counseling. David, the shepherd boy with his flocks, had psychological insight and was able to help an emotionally disturbed person. Rulers were spoken of as being counselors and overseers of the flock. Jesus had a vital ministry to individuals, and the deacons who were laymen worked in very close relationships as they helped people. In the work of the great Apostle to the Gentiles, Paul was mainly concerned with propagating a message; yet, his letters reveal close relationships with people.

A favored term used to describe the counselor is "pastor" or "shepherd." Used in this manner, there is an indication that the term "pastoral" describes the shepherding activity rather than the person who does the task. The humble layman engaged in some task of trying to help another can become involved in shepherding activity or pastoral counseling.

The ministry of counseling, so important in that bygone day, is important today. The one who said to his followers, "Go ye into all the world, and preach the gospel to every creature" (Mark 16:15) also spoke to the discredited disciple on the seashore and asked for a reaffirmation of his love by saying, "Lovest thou me?" (John 21:17*a*). In response to the reaffirmed love, Jesus commanded his disciple, "Feed my sheep" (John 21:17*b*). The great task of shepherding is the heritage of the Christian church. The Old Testament bears the divine example of God himself of whom it is said, "He shall feed his flock like a shepherd: he shall gather the lambs with his arm, and carry them in his bosom, and shall gently lead those that are with young." (Isa. 40:11).

Moreover, as we think of the emphases of the Bible, we need to remember that the whole of Christian tradition has agreed upon the identity of the one who came in New Testament times as the one spoken of by the Old Testament prophet when he said, "His name shall be called . . . Counsellor" (Isa. 9:6).

2. *Personality in the Drama of Life*

IN THE ANCIENT Greek theater, men played all of the parts. To attract attention to the characters, the actors wore high-heeled shoes, padded shoulders, and masks. The mask indicated to the audience the character being portrayed. The mouth of the mask was shaped like a megaphone and served as an amplifier to throw the actor's voice out into the audience. By this means the actor "sounded through."

The word used for mask later came to mean personality. The word "personality" connotes three associated ideas. The first is appearance. Then comes the idea of the role which the person plays in life. This is followed, thirdly, by the thought of "sounding through." So the personality is the vehicle through which contact is made with other people. The three ideas are always inherent in any thought about personality.

Environment's Slave or Master

With the development of studies in the areas of the social sciences, people have become increasingly aware of the importance of the individual's environment. In a study reported recently, Sheldon and Eleanor Glueck developed a system of predicting criminal behavior. After many years of careful investigation, they came up with the startling idea that criminal behavior could be as accurately forecast as an insurance company figures the odds on accidents or deaths. Studying elaborate statistics on thousands of criminals, the Gluecks isolated key factors that could be used in the prediction of delinquency. They say the five highly decisive factors are: father's discipline, mother's supervision, father's affection toward his son, mother's affection, cohesiveness of the family. It is claimed that these environmental factors are so important that predictions made, using them as a basis and compared with the behavior of two thousand delinquents in New York, were found to be 90 per cent accurate.[1]

Similarly, psychologists have emphasized environment. Freudian psychologists particularly underline the importance of the early days of development and the emphasis on such things as breast feeding, toilet training, mother-child relationships, and associated early experiences. Freud's emphasis upon the early days of development has been highlighted in the statement "The drama of life to Freud is but a repetition of the plot of infancy."

In more recent writings a new note is appearing, which stresses that men are not necessarily pawns of environmental influences. Counselors working in the practical field have long reflected this idea and emphasized the importance of the individual's decision-making.

An illustration which may help is that of a plane equipped with a modern mechanical pilot. The human pilot sits behind his mechanical counterpart and may, at any time, take control of the machine. The engine and the fuselage of the plane correspond to the human body, and the automatic pilot is analogous to the responses developed by environmental influences. However, there is a time when man takes control and makes life-changing decisions. The great psychiatrist Viktor Frankl in his book *The Doctor and the Soul* states: "Thus, man is by no means merely a product of heredity and environment. There is a third element: decision. Man ultimately decides for himself!" [2] However, the complicating factor in all this is that man does not always recognize the factors influencing his decisions.

The Psychological Insult

Stern, a famous psychologist, once said that science has dealt man a number of insults. He stressed the "psychological insult," which was seen as the blow dealt to man's self-love when he discovers he is not master of his own house, but, in a large measure, is motivated by the unconscious forces of his personality. The idea of an unconscious segment of the mind so significant in personality patterns was revolutionary when first popularized by Freud but is now widely accepted.

Levels of the Mind

For convenience, it may be said that, in the view of dynamic psychology, the mind functions at three levels: the conscious, the preconscious, and the unconscious. These are not to be thought of as watertight compartments or immovable divisions. Very frequently one will shade off into the other, and it is difficult to be dogmatic about the specific details of each of the levels.

The *conscious* is the segment of the mind concerned with immediate awareness. At this moment you know you are reading, and your attention wanders off to any number of things of which you are immediately aware.

Preconscious or foreconscious is the word used to describe the material in the mind recallable by focusing attention upon it. Examples of this would be the name of a friend, the address of a house in which you live, the mental image of someone you know. Each of these things is now conscious. A moment ago it was preconscious, but available for recall.

The *unconscious* is a vast storehouse of ideas, wishes, and emotional shocks which once were conscious but now are relegated to the unconscious. Within it are many of the primitive strivings and forgotten memories and experiences of earlier days. Carrington gives an excellent summary of the unconscious when he says:

The whole pattern of the Freudian concept is built on the existence and power of this deep unconscious part of the mind, without which the field of consciousness would be so cluttered up with useless material that the ego could not function properly. But however necessary the unconscious part of the mind may be for normal psychic function, it may provide some complex problems when psychic function is disturbed.[3]

One of the analogies used to illustrate the unconscious is the iceberg, six-sevenths of which is submerged, leaving only one-seventh above the water. The larger six-sevenths represents the powerful unconscious, proportionately greater than the conscious area.

The Nature of the Unconscious

The unconscious may be summed up in the three words: *primitive, purposive,* and *pushing.* Consideration of each of these serves to indicate significant aspects of the unconscious.

The primitive unconscious.—Within the unconscious are forces which were of great importance in the infancy of civilization but are often troublesome in a twentieth-century culture. Walter Murdoch illustrates this in his essay "Beasts in the Basement," where he tells of inheriting a house from an eccentric aunt. At the reading of the will, he discovers to his dismay that he is obliged, under its terms, to keep alive the animals housed in the cellar. The motley assortment includes a tiger brought from India by his grandfather, a parrot given by his Aunt Celina, a donkey donated by Uncle Henry, and sundry other animals. Each animal has come from some deceased relative. Compelled by the terms of the legacy to keep this menagerie alive, Murdoch tries to conceal their existence, but there are some difficult moments. While entertaining friends, a lion roars, a parrot screeches, and a donkey brays. Murdoch shuffles his feet, clears his throat, or, in some way, tries to distract his guests' attention. The writer interprets his story:

Now the figure of the private menagerie, to represent the subterranean workings of our minds, is so obvious that I expect it has been scandalously overworked. Caged within us, and kept in normal circumstances invisible to others and even to ourselves, are numerous wild primitive urges, tendencies, instincts, call them what you will, which we have inherited from savage forebears. Civilized society implies their repression, but they are there all the time, alive and active. In certain circumstances, an old ancestral tiger of aggressiveness will wake in me and roar; try to make me do something distasteful to me, and an ancient mule will plant his hoofs firmly on the ground and refuse to budge; touch my vanity, and an atavistic porcupine will raise all his bristles; tickle one of my appetites, and you will hear the grunting of an immemorial pig; try to argue me out of an unreasonable prejudice, and a patriarchal donkey will lift his head to heaven and bray.[4]

Lest it should be felt that this is just the product of the essayist's imagination, it is well to remember that in the New Testament there are references to this part of personality. In Ephesians 4:22 we read, "That ye put off concerning the former conversation the old man, which is corrupt according to the deceitful lusts. Similarly, in the Pauline writings the word "flesh" frequently seems to have the idea of primitive forces within man.

The purposive unconscious.—This primitive part of the mind, seeking self-preservation above everything else, is fundamentally self-centered and tries to get the best deal for the individual, even though he is unaware of its activity. A man asked by his wife to mow the lawn, works at it for a short time and then announces that he is too tired to finish and stretches out on the sofa to recuperate. A short time later, when a friend calls to know if he can play golf, his strength is miraculously restored; and he goes out to play a strenuous eighteen holes.

Functional illnesses, which have no physical basis, are manifestations of the strange power of the unconscious. The soldier in a difficult spot has a paralyzed leg that necessitates his evacuation; the housewife, tired of the never ending routine, gets a sick headache; and the preacher in a difficult church situation loses his voice. Such things, though painful, exhausting, and done unconsciously, do offer a way of escape. They represent the purposive workings of the unconscious in transforming a mental conflict into a physical symptom.

The pushing unconscious.—Think back to the illustration of the iceberg. The wind may be blowing in one direction while the iceberg appears to be moving in the opposite direction. The reason is that the pressure of the wind is being brought to bear upon the one-seventh above the water, and the sea currents are acting upon the submerged six-sevenths. So it is with the *pushing* forces of the unconscious.

Vance Packard, in his best seller *The Hidden Persuaders*, tells of "motivational research," which seeks to influence people at the unconscious level and motivate them to purchase the advertiser's goods. Much research went into discovering why people wanted higher powered automobiles. One investigator came up with the idea that it was to express aggressive impulses. An immediate response of auto merchandisers was to stress that the driver of their automobile could just push down the throttle and experience a surge of power whenever he wanted to.

The unconscious serves to complicate living by repressing unacceptable ideas. This involves the unwitting process by which people relegate painful memories and conflicts into the unconscious. Leslie D. Weatherhead uses a rather apt illustration:

These forgotten, and psychologically traumatic, incidents, charged with repressed emotion, are not allowed into consciousness because they are obnoxious to the patient's peace of mind, to his self-respect, to his ideal of himself, and so forth. But they do not lie dormant in the unconscious mind as mud lies at the bottom of a pond. Although withheld from consciousness, they revenge themselves, as it were, by expressing their energies in terms of mental symptoms of anxiety, or fear, or physical symptoms. . . .

To keep the analogy of the pond, we may imagine that the mud at the bottom contains fermenting material which sends up bubbles to the surface. So, on the surface of the mind, symptoms like the emotion of fear or the pain of asthma may be experienced, as different from their origin as bubbles are different from mud, but also as consequent.[5]

Repressions in the unconscious may serve to complicate behavior in church people; and explanations offered for conduct are often far from the real reason, even though most sincerely believed.

However, if repression represents the means by which the operations of the unconscious are complicated, the mental mechanism of *sublimation* presents the means of utilizing the strong and driving forces of the unconscious. Sublimation is defined as "refinement or redirection of the energy belonging to a primitive tendency into new noninherited channels."[6] A common illustration might be that of a community settled on a hillside. After prolonged rains, a destructive stream of water comes running down, tearing away the foundations of the buildings. If someone were to conceive the idea of rechanneling the water, sending it down over the side of the hill, it could run to the farm lands and be used to irrigate the crops and to make the earth fruitful. It has been said that while psychology teaches sublimation, it takes religion to put meaning into it. Religious motivations are often of vital importance in the process of sublimating unconscious energies into new creative channels.

Checks and Balances Within Personality

Within personality there is a complex organization in which Freud saw three dynamically interacting systems. These he called the id, the ego, and the superego. Jestingly, the whole of psychology has been defined as "the study of the id by the odd."

The id is the first system of personality representing the primitive, pushing, unregulated urges within the individual's life. These urges live by the *pleasure principle* and are the striving part of personality seeking only for its own pleasure, irrespective of what happens to others.

Superego, Freud's second system, is sometimes called the ego ideal or the value system; and, for our purpose, it may be said to be essentially the same as conscience. It represents the accepted standards and the ideals toward which we strive.

From what has been already said, one might conceive that man is a victim of either his primitive nature or his lofty ideals. The limerick states it:

> There was a handsome young amigo,
> Whose badly overworked libido,
> Gave vent to his "id,"
> And his personality slid,
> All because of a weak superego.

Rather unfortunately, this would-be poet minimized the all-important third system of personality, the ego.

Between the crude, primitive, selfish, demanding forces of the id on the one hand and the standards, ideals, and the goals of the superego on the other stands the all-important third system called the ego. The balance between the id and the superego is maintained by the ego, which represents the executive force of personality, the deciding factor which says "I will" or "I will not."

An illustration of the relationship of the three personality systems may be seen in a bronco-riding contest at a rodeo. The horse is held in the chute until the rider gets into the saddle; seated on the rider's shoulder is an elf-like person who whispers instructions in his ear. The horse is then released, and the battle between man and beast begins. The wild horse represents the unregulated urges, seeking to rid themselves of all control; the little person whispering instructions to the rider is the superego or value system; while the rider of the wild horse may be likened to the ego. The rider is trying to listen to the advice of the superego, control the bucking bronco, called the id, and at the same time remain conscious of the external world—the excited, cheering, watching crowd.

In relating to people, we are trying to help develop their ego strength so that they can handle their primitive urges and also have sensible ideals for their lives. Some people who are emotionally sick do not have well-formed superegos; therefore, they live their lives at the mercy of the primitive drives within their personalities. The psychopathic or sociopathic personality is an illustration of this. Such a personality has no depth of emotional life, no sense of guilt, and his whole attitude toward life is indicative of a poorly developed superego. On the other hand, in a religious setting, a person's superego may be overdeveloped, causing guilt out of proportion to the misdemeanor which results in a constant confessing of sins. Such a person has no apparent capacity to accept the full message of forgiveness through Christ. In seeking to help people manage their lives, it is best to help them develop within themselves the capacity to handle their own problems and to keep a sensible balance between the urges of their id and the demands of their superego.

Mental Mechanisms

In the early days of motoring, the driver was very proud of being able to shift gears without clashing them. His skill at knowing when and how to shift was an important factor in rating his driving ability. The modern automobile, with its automatic transmission, has removed this consideration in driving skill. Like the automatic transmission which, in consideration of the power of the engine, the grade of the hill, and the pressure on the accelerator, engages the appropriate gear without the driver's help, so there are self-corrective devices within the personality. The demands of the id and superego and the permissions of the ego are often automatically adjusted by mental mechanisms or dynamisms.

One of the most frequently utilized mechanisms is *rationalization*. The logical or carefully reasoned arguments which are produced in justification of behavior are often far from the truth but often seem more acceptable than the real reasons. An aggressive atheist produces a series of powerful arguments against religion and gives a flattering picture of his intellectual prowess. Investigation shows he had once been jilted by a devout Sunday school teacher. The emotional upset therefrom was the real reason for his antagonism toward the church; but it was much more satisfying to his ego to parade his so-called intelligence.

Trying to make up for personal inadequacy may lead to the utilization of the dynamism of *phantasy*. Actual activity may be replaced with imagined activity. Most people have been guilty of daydreaming at some time or another. Sometimes this can be productive, as it is in creative imagination, but all too frequently it is a technique for the evasion of responsibility.

There are at least two types of phantasy—the conquering hero and the suffering hero. In the first, the unsuccessful individual sees himself as the captain of industry; the physically weak as the muscular wrestler; the fainthearted as the great and courageous soldier. The suffering hero is seen in the person who does not worry over a personal inferiority because he sees himself as a willing martyr to his awful fate. While everyone needs to escape temporarily from some of life's starkest realities, if the individual resorts to phantasy too frequently, he increasingly loses touch with the world of reality; and adequate personality adjustment may be hindered.

The mechanism of *projection* enables the individual to see his own faults in other people. When he transgresses, it is not very important; but the same misdemeanor seen in another person is repulsive. The Bible story of King David who stole another man's wife demonstrates projection. Later, the prophet Nathan tells him of a man who took his neighbor's ewe lamb, and David blazes in indignation, insisting that the culprit be punished. He is amazed when Nathan says, "Thou art the man."

Compensation, as implied in the normal use of the word, is the mechanism whereby we make up for what we see as defects in our lives. The procedure may be objectionable as in the small person who, by various means such as talking in a loud voice, gains a feeling of importance by calling attention to himself. On the other hand, compensation may be commendable, as with the person who, in an effort to make up for his shortcomings, develops new and valuable capacities. A classic illustration is Demosthenes who, with pebbles in his mouth cried out against the voice of the waves until he conquered his stammering and stuttering, became the greatest orator of antiquity.

The Unruly Emotions

In primitive society the emotional reactions of the individual were of great value. In a state of fear, accessions of strength enabled man to face the physical threats of the jungle about him. Such emotional reactions may still be of help in emergencies. During a fire one man carried to safety a heavy safe containing valuable papers. Later, it took three men to put it back in place. Rather unfortunately, however, these emotions easily get out of gear because they are primitive reactions which do not necessarily help the individual in a modern society, where he is fairly safe from external danger.

The difficult process of handling the emotional life comes from *internal conflicts* which may give rise to an uneasy condition known as anxiety. Menninger says anxiety is a kind of red flag, a warning that something is wrong in the relationship of the ego, the superego, and the id.

When the emotional life gets out of gear, an individual's reactions may be classified under one of several headings. The milder forms are called neurotic or psychoneurotic. In these, the person may react inappropriately or out of all proportion to the facts of the situation; become depressed over long periods of time; tend to perform certain acts over and over without any real reason; have unreasonable and exaggerated fears, experience bodily illnesses without any physical basis; and continually worry about everything in general.

The more serious types of emotional difficulties are called psychoses. The main distinction between the psychotic and the neurotic reaction is that the psychotic individual has long periods when he is completely out of touch with reality. While the neurotic may be aware of his illness and may function fairly well in society, the psychotic is unconcerned and unsuccessful. The neurotic will be anxious and depressed and have some bodily symptoms; the psychotic will have hallucinations and distorted emotional reactions. He will probably need institutional care, but the neurotic may be helped by counseling and psychotherapy. A simple criterion for the layman to use in distinguishing serious types of emotional reaction will be found in chapter 9.

Personality is a complex mechanism that easily gets out of gear. The influences of environment, the primitive, pushing and purposive unconscious which often mask the real motivations of life, and the checks and balances of the pleasure-seeking id, the scrupulous superego, and the executive ego present many possibilities of maladjustment. Accommodating to these pressures are the dynamisms such as rationalization, excusing reality; phantasy and projection, distorted reality; and compensation, atoning for reality.

Unruly emotions enter to complicate the picture, and the psychoneurosis or even the phychosis may represent the individual's surrender in the desperate situation. The layman will never become involved with psychotic people or even a serious psychoneurotic. However, in milder forms of difficulty he may be of great help, as will be seen in the following chapters.

3. *The Layman's Special Ministry*

ONE OF THE tragedies of modern church life is the inadequate use of the layman. Sight has been lost of one of the most significant aspects of the Reformation. Before the Reformation it was thought that the clergy had a vocation or calling from God which was denied the lay members of the church, but Luther extended the idea to mean that every man was called of God to his vocation. The expression "vocational guidance" comes directly from Luther. The emphasis upon God's calling to all forms of work led Luther to claim that no matter how lowly the task, it is important to God. In his earthy way, he stated that the milkmaid and the carter of manure were doing a work more pleasing to God than that of the monk singing psalms in the monastery. It follows from this that the layman's contacts with people in all his activities of life should be interpreted as opportunities for service to God and to his fellow man.

The Untapped Resource

Referring to the almost impossible task confronting a minister in his effort to lessen the present-day erosion of home life, John C. Wynn makes a plea for the utilization of lay men and women:

No pastor alone . . . could hope to minister adequately to the needs of his parish families. In so huge an assignment he needs help. Unless he recruits and trains others who can aid in carrying on this family ministry, his pastoral work cannot succeed. Among the homes on the church roll are persons who can share in the task.[1]

Thus comes a long overdue recognition of the possibility of laymen becoming valuable allies to the pastor in the best tradition of the reformed faith.

It is not necessary to have a special office, a receptionist, an elaborate setting, and a couch to be able to help people. It is not even necessary to have specialized training. L. J. Moreno has bluntly stated that the personality of the counselor is the skill.

In chapter 1, it was noted that people in Bible times helped others without technical knowledge or special settings. David on the hillside, Paul in prison, and the wise men at the city gate all had remarkable interpersonal relationships, despite the setting within which they functioned and the complete absence of any formal methods as we know them today.

The potentiality of lay people has been dramatized by the experience of marriage counseling services in England. Faced with a shortage of trained personnel, the Marriage Guidance Movement uses lay men and women. They are carefully selected, screened and trained, then set to work within a team. Possibly the most illuminating discovery comes from the evaluation of the psychiatric supervisors who, after working with both lay and professional groups of counselors:

admit that in the quality of work done there has been no difference at all between the lay counselors and the professional counselors. They simply had to admit against their prejudices that properly trained lay counselors who were properly selected in the first place can do every bit as good a job as professional counselors.[2]

From the academic point of view these discoveries are most disconcerting, but they open up new and exciting possibilities for the utilization of laymen in the work of interpersonal relationships.

Experience in institutional settings has shown that there are often individuals who will not bother to go to a counseling center where highly trained professional help is available. They will prefer, rather, to take their difficulties to some respected teacher, staff member, or a psychologically unsophisticated person. While these counselors are not psychologically trained, they apparently have the gifts of personality which enable them to relate to others.

Even if it were possible, it would be ridiculous to exclude these people from the counseling field.

In the counseling area within the church setting, the layman may have an advantage over the professional religious worker. People may be reluctant to talk about their problems to the pastor because they want to save face or they may see him as the authoritarian preacher who has such high ideals that he will not understand their frailties. The wise layman is able to see a special opportunity to help; and, if the matter is serious enough to warrant it, he will encourage his counselee to talk with the pastor.

Informal Contacts

Availability is of great significance in counseling, and the layman may have a distinct advantage in this area. In his book on pastoral care, Belgum discusses the counseling ministry of the hospital chaplain. He shows that an important person in this situation is the nurse, who may be with the patient for as long as eight hours a day. Consequently, it often happens that she is the one to whom the patient opens his heart and pours out his fears and apprehensions. This happens even though there are many highly specialized people such as the doctor, the psychiatrist, the social worker, and the chaplain, who had been trained for this type of service. The chaplain sometimes feels bad because the patient has told his spiritual problem to the nurse rather than sending for him. The situation arises because the chaplain is available *officially* while the nurse is available *practically*.

Similarly, availability is important for the Sunday school superintendent, the Sunday school teacher, or the leader in youth work. The layman must constantly watch for possibilities for helpful contacts. The very nature of his work brings him into close contact with people. He calls on them in their homes and meets them in various gatherings. He goes to socials, picnics, and other church functions. In many ways the lay worker is much closer to the people than the minister of the church and, consequently, will often have unusual opportunities. Like the nurse in the hospital setting, he is *practically* available.

The informal type of ministry was significantly dramatized in the life and work of our Lord Jesus Christ. He looked into a tree and saw Zacchaeus and called him down to talk with him; he met a sinful woman by a wayside well; he talked with two who trudged along the way to Emmaus and listened as they recounted the story of their disappointments. A great amount of Jesus' ministry was spent in individual contacts. This was so despite his sense of mission which drove him on to work while it was yet day. In like manner, the layman in the busy life of the twentieth century will have many contacts with people which may prove to be very rewarding.

A man who is now an outstanding counselor tells of an experience at a church social where he fell into conversation with a young woman. Though they had been attending the same church, he had never talked to her before. As they chatted about trivialities, she suddenly turned to him and said, "Do you ever do counseling?" The man, somewhat embarrassed, replied that he did and made an appointment to see the young lady. The experience helped to launch him on a professional counseling career. Chance contacts in church life can open doors to meaningful opportunities to help others.

Organizational Relationships

The modern church is highly organized, but still mainly staffed with laymen. Much of the effectiveness of contacts within the organization will depend upon the way in which these laymen view their work. A church organization may be thought of as a way in which people can be manipulated and made to follow the plans of their leader. This is organization at its poorest level. On the other hand, it may be seen as a framework within which people can grow and develop, as they are led to follow the plans of their leader. This is organization at its best.

To help in the growth process, attention must be focused upon the individual within the group. Good leaders have always emphasized the individual. Norman Rockwell writes of his experience when painting the portrait of President Eisenhower:

The general and I didn't discuss politics or the campaign. Mostly we talked about painting and fishing. But what I remember most about the hour and a half I spent with him was the way he gave me all his attention. He was listening to *me* and talking to *me*, just as if he hadn't a care in the world, hadn't been through the trials of a political convention, wasn't on the brink of a presidential campaign.[3]

The President had had much to do with organization and large groups of people. His success as a military leader and later as President of the United States was probably due in a great measure to his consciousness of the importance of the individual within the group.

The closeness of the lay leader to those within his organization aids in counseling. A good Sunday school teacher knows the members of his group and can often see developing difficulties. A class member whose attendance becomes sporadic, shows signs of stress in the class session, or in discussion reveals an attitude of resentment or disillusionment, may be seen as one in need of help. The leader of the youth group sees who dates whom, how free they are with members of the opposite sex, attitudes towards parents, feelings about school and authority. In this essential mating period, degrees of involvement may be discerned and trouble headed off. Children in Sunday school often talk freely and tell that Daddy stayed away all the week, Grandmother is staying with them and she and Mother are having quarrels, and so on. The astute and perceptive leader is again in a position to see the distress signals and to go into action.

Teaching activities can provide openings for counseling experiences. Well organized Sunday school lessons are prepared in consideration of class members' needs. With a small homogeneous group, the teacher seeks to apply the lesson to the experiences of the class members. The teacher may sometimes speak in the first person, stating what she said to her children, how her husband pleased or annoyed her, how she felt about the relatives who dropped in on her unexpectedly. Though this type of teaching might annoy the perfectionist who is considering teaching techniques, the woman who sits in her class feels that the teacher understands something of the frustrating experiences through which she herself is passing. Consequently, she is often more willing to talk with her teacher than she would be to other people.

One of the most profitable activities in which a layman can engage is home visitation. However, there are many callers on the modern home, most of whom are trying in some way to exploit the householder. If the church worker only thinks of the individual as a prospect for his organization, he may have unwittingly joined the ranks of the exploiters. He must aim at establishing a relationship of confidence and friendship with an emphasis on understanding the person visited. Too many church workers feel they have to defend the good name of the church, if it is criticized, or belligerently attack the unresponsive householder. The caller should follow the lead conversation, giving the one visited an opportunity to express himself. As the visitor undertakes his task with respect for the other's personality and leavens all that he does with Christian love, he helps develop growth potential.

Because most of the workers within a church organization are volunteers, there is a tendency for trouble to come through displaced emotions. *Displacement* is a mental mechanism concerned with the shifting of emotional energy from a sensitive area to another where it can be better tolerated. Thorpe calls this the "kick the cat" mechanism and beautifully illustrates it:

An executive who has had a quarrel with his wife at breakfast becomes irritable and critical of his secretary, who in turn snaps at her husband at dinnertime with the result that he spanks their son for a minor misdemeanor. Again, a child may go into his baby sister's room and pinch her until she screams with rage and throws her doll violently on the floor. In this instance the doll brings the cycle to a close and lies still until the storm passes.[4]

A great preacher has been credited with saying, "Resist the devil and he will fly from you, resist the deacon and he will fly at you." It may be that the deacon really wants to fly at his boss or at his wife but cannot do this and preserve his status. The layman in the group will be able to help much more if he perceives the mechanism which is at work.

Thorpe again helps by describing the process of group therapy:

In general, although larger groups have been used successfully, six to ten persons meet once or twice a week under the direction of a trained leader or therapist. Either guided or unstructured discussions of personal problems form the basis for group dynamics, in which situations the person sees himself in relation to others as well as seeing others in their interactions with each other.[5]

Committee work presents unusual opportunities for group therapy. Within this more intimate group, members will often let their defenses down and express themselves more freely. Committee members with some psychological insight can utilize the situation so that it can be of tremendous value. From being a thing to be dreaded, a committee meeting can become a therapeutic experience. Members can stimulate each other and the interaction lead to shared ideals and a willingness to compromise and cooperate. Price states the reactions within the therapeutic group:

This atmosphere demands self-analysis and insight on the part of all participants. "Why do I react negatively or hastily to certain individuals?" and "What are my motives for being here?" are typical questions. This group-centered approach implies equality on the part of all present. Thus mutual respect will grow. "Did I 'pigeon-hole' that person before I really knew him?" and "How can I help him to grow?" are typical reactions.[6]

The layman who develops skills in group leadership and utilizes group dynamics will have the stimulating experience of watching the development of personality potential.

Protestantism has often been successful to the extent to which it has used its lay people. Among evangelical churches, it is insisted that the layman has not only a right but also an obligation to speak to people about their relationship with God. If this is so, he can just as confidently be asked to help people in their human relationships. By the development of psychological insight and a sensitivity to human relations, the layman may yet make his greatest contribution to church life and ultimately to the kingdom of God.

4. What Your Listening Does for People

SOLOMON said there was a time for every purpose which is under heaven, and there was "a time to keep silence, and a time to speak" (Eccl. 3:7). Most church leaders agree that there is a time to speak and feel it is a tragedy if there is not some sound filling the air, preferably that of their own voices. But Solomon puts the capacity to keep silent on equal status with the capacity to speak. In the specific instructions given to the wise men who were the counselors of ancient Israel, it was twice stated that they must be willing to listen. Later, in the ministry of Jesus, he said, "He that hath ears to hear, let him hear."

Unfortunately, this is an age in which people do not bother to listen. It has been said that listening is the lost *L* in learning. Educational emphasis has moved from the pupil who was seen and not heard to the student who is encouraged to participate and express himself. This leads to the idea that to speak is more important than to listen. A bore has been described as "someone who keeps on talking after you have thought of something clever to say." The poet has expressed a similar thought:

> I bend a sympathetic ear
> To other people's woes,
> However dull it is to hear
> Their real or fancied throes.
> I pay, to every gloomy line,
> Attention undiminished,
> Because I plan to start on mine
> The minute theirs are finished.[1]

An apt illustration of this was contained in a Roman Catholic paper. The writer, speaking about penance, suggested one for the proud, "You will not talk about yourself for one day." Many people would consider this a terrible punishment.

It is not possible for everybody to speak all the time. Someone must listen. One experimenter actually developed a scheme of counseling in which the counselee spoke into a tape recorder and played it back to see how he sounded. George Orwell's *Nineteen Eighty-Four* depicts the Communist regime as having an all-seeing eye in every home. Perhaps this idea might be refined so that a mechanical ear can be added to each residence for the unfortunate citizen who feels that he must have someone to listen to him.

People have a special need for a listening ear. When two people are talking, it is natural to assume that the speaker is trying to communicate information to the listener. However, very often people talk without conveying ideas or concepts. Much conversation is mere wordiness and has little intellectual content. People seldom speak to each other to convey information. They merely want an audience. The reason for this is very involved and complicated. In this chapter, an examination will be made of some of the reasons people need to talk and, consequently, are helped when another person is willing to listen.

People Need to Break Out of Their Isolation

In his book on maturity, Overstreet points out that in a special sense man is born alone, and as he grows he has to develop "word-linkages" with the world. "Speech, again, is that through which we most commonly seek to escape our skin-enclosed isolation and to enter into a community of experience." [2] Willingness to listen to people builds a bridge so they can enter into this community of experience.

A foreign student, who came to America in 1954, stayed in the dormitory of a theological seminary. On the first morning after his arrival, he was shaving in the communal bathroom when a fellow student stumbled in. He greeted the foreign student with "What do you say?" Since the foreign student had never heard this kind of greeting, he was somewhat puzzled as to how he should respond. After thinking for a while he said, "I beg your pardon." The American repeated his statement. Pondering for a few moments, the foreign student answered, "Excuse me, I didn't say anything." The American looked with a startled expression and muttered something like "Skip it" and went on with his shaving. Later, the foreign student was able to see that he had been led astray by a colloquialism. All this man was attempting to say was, "I am another human being. I can see that you are rather lonely and I am trying to communicate with you." So it is with much conversation. When one person asks, "How are you today," he is not asking for a health report. He is simply seeking to open up channels of communication.

Isolation can be threatening. Though there is much speculation about the wonderful possibility of being away from the maddening crowd, the inherent sense of incompleteness causes people to long for the company of others. It is in the company of, and reaction to, others that we discover our real selves. Johnson has postulated this in his interpersonal axiom for personality development, which he feels takes place in the interaction of one person to another. Helen Keller is a dramatic illustration of this. Deaf, dumb, and blind, she was cut off from the world. Her dedicated teacher worked and struggled until she managed to tap out a message on Helen's hand, which at last established communication. The tremendous growth potential was released and Helen Keller developed into one of the great personalities of our day. Similarly, the counselor who is willing to listen is opening up communication which helps the counselee to escape from his isolation and to discover his own potential for growth.

Troubles Put into Words Often Disappear

Some psychologists have made much of the fact that the capacity to imagine differentiates man from other forms of animal life. While this capacity to imagine is a tremendous asset to man, it also has its liabilities.

There are many people who have a tendency to withdraw from

the realities of life and to live in an imaginary world. Professionals use the term "fantasy" to describe this escape mechanism. If a person resorts too much to fantasy, he can easily become confused as to what is *fact* and what is *fantasy*. Walter Mitty, in the famous story by Thurber, was dominated by his wife and mother-in-law. By lapsing into fantasy, he saw himself as a great surgeon, a broncobuster, a sea captain, or some other heroic figure, rather than the poor henpecked person he really was.

The test of verbalization is an excellent way of clarifying one's thought processes. When a person has a chance to verbalize his thinking, to bring it out in the open, to hear it, and then to see how another responds to it, he often sees the irrationality of his thought processes.

Very often as a person begins to express an idea, thought, or concept which does not correspond to reality, he will begin to realize, even at the moment of expression, just how incorrect he is. This was confirmed some years ago by an experiment carried out by a large company which provided counselors for its employees. The counselors had no power to change things or intervene in the affairs of management, but were instructed to give the employees opportunity to talk freely about their complaints. Following this procedure, the counselors found that one of two things frequently happened. First, an employee annoyed about his work situation frequently discovered that when he talked to a sympathetic and nonjudgmental listener, his problem was not what he first imagined it to be. He often found that his real trouble lay in some other area. Secondly, these counselors found that the complaints often evaporated as they talked about them. As the employee brooded, his complaints grew to amazing proportions. When he had an opportunity to verbalize and express these complaints, he began to realize their unimportance.

Therefore, verbalizing and expressing thoughts often provides a corrective, enabling people to see things in their true perspective. The process is not inevitable, but its possibility is a reason why people need someone who will listen—someone who will not pass judgment but will listen sympathetically.

People Need to Express Emotions as well as Thoughts

When a person in a frustrated frame of mind speaks to another person, the emotional content of what he says is of far more importance than the thought content. From this it follows that people's statements cannot be taken at face value. Many of the problems in church life come from trying to hold one responsible for something he said in an angry mood.

An example of this need to express emotion is the loving wife who goes to a lot of trouble to prepare her husband's favorite meal. She cooks a steak, baked potatoes, and all the trimmings. The table is beautifully arranged and everything just as she knows he likes it. As he enters the door, she kisses him and says, "Look what I have prepared for you."

The husband walks over, looks at it, and says: "Why ever on earth did you fix a meal like this? You know I don't like T-bone steak. I never did. Why are you wasting our money? You know our budget won't stand food like this."

If the wife takes these statements at face value, there may be domestic discord. However, if she thinks for a while, she may realize her husband is saying something else. He is not *really* saying, "I don't like T-bone." He is saying, "I had a rotten day at the office today," or "I went to the drugstore and the clerk gypped me," or "I was doing thirty-five miles per hour and the police caught and booked me."

It has been suggested that if the wife takes his statement at face value and becomes involved in an argument about the merits of the meal, the marriage might be wrecked over a T-bone steak. But if she is wise enough to accept what he has to say and suggests that she fix some beans for him, there is a good possibility he will say, "Well, since you have the steak, I might as well eat it."

The church leader must listen for the emotional communication as well as the intellectual. When he is approached by an irate member of his organization who is complaining bitterly, he will query silently: "What is the feeling that he is trying to express here, and what does it indicate about his attitude toward his job, toward me, or toward somebody else?"

The Expression of Troublesome Emotions Sometimes
Causes Them to Lose Their Intensity

Emotional intensities tend to build up rapidly. An illustration of this is the old hose blocked off at one end. As the pressures become greater it is evident that something must happen. Ultimately, the hose gives way in its weakest spots and the water squirts out. People react in much the same way. Emotional pressures develop when people brood and worry. They must find some means of release. Like the blocked hose, without release they will erupt in the most vulnerable area of the personality.

The counselor should be mature enough not to become personally involved or defensive during these emotional outbursts. If he is objective and permissive, he will provide a channel for the draining of the emotion. One writer uses the illustration of a teakettle over a flame. If left with the lid and cap on, it will explode. However, when the cap is taken off the spout and some steam allowed to escape, the pressure is reduced—some teakettles will even whistle.

Speech has been described as man's most ready safety valve. Counselors have found that when people are allowed to talk about the things that are worrying them, the emotional intensity often subsides. In psychological terminology this is called catharsis. In its original usage in the Greek drama, catharsis literally meant a purging of the emotions. Shakespeare apparently understood something of the value of speech as an outlet for emotional pressure, for he wrote:

> Give sorrow words: the grief that does not speak
> Whispers the o'er-fraught heart and bids it break.[3]

Confessional Experience Can Be Psychologically
and Religiously Significant

Down through the years the church has intuitively understood that people need to talk about things which are worrying them. Such an idea has been institutionalized by the Roman Catholic Church. Because of the implications involved within the Roman

Catholic confessional, most Protestants have turned aside from it. However, it is interesting to note that Martin Luther was prepared to keep elements of the confessional, although he rejected much other Roman Catholic doctrine. "He . . . looked upon confession as useful, provided it was not institutionalized." [4] From a psychological viewpoint, it is now realized that a priestly setting is not necessary but may be a detriment to true confession and that a minister or layman in a permissive atmosphere might offer better opportunities for such an experience.

Concerning the good which comes from confession, Leslie D. Weatherhead [5] outlines four great values:

It cleanses the mind. Writing from the viewpoint of mental health, Groves and Groves dwell on the importance of confession, saying that one of the reasons why religion is helpful for the development of mental health is that religion makes confessional experiences available. [6] In his book on alcoholism, Clinebell answers the criticisms of Alcoholics Anonymous members' standing to confess their shortcomings before their fellow members:

Verbalization of one's past escapades before a sympathetic audience is actually part of the cathartic process of working through one's guilt feelings. The fact that a person can now tell in public of experiences which a few months before were too painful for him even to admit to himself is a sign of real progress. [7]

Confession relieves the conscience. People will say, "If I've been able to talk to someone about this thing, and he has been able to assure me of God's forgiveness, then certainly, I can go to God and tell him about it."

Confession ends the loneliness of pretense. We have previously noted that people who are conscious of their shortcomings very often build up facades to try to justify themselves in the face of the world in which they live. In confession, there is an opening of the channels and the isolation of this pretense is broken down.

Confession opens the way through which there can come an experience of faith in Jesus Christ.

Students at a university complained that jukeboxes in the student union interfered with their studying, so records were produced which gave three-minute silence for a dime. Some were played so often that they produced noisy needle scratches and had to be replaced. People were willing to pay for a few moments' silence.

A recent newspaper cartoon had a woman telling her psychiatrist, "If only my husband would listen to me as you do." It might well be that if more of us were willing to sit still, be silent and listen, there would be many people who would not have to pay to get a few moments of silence or a listening ear.

5. The Art of Listening

LISTENING may be thought of as a sensory process by which the sound waves reach the ear, pass through a complicated apparatus to the auditory nerve where neural currents take the impulse to the brain. But one can hear without listening. Listening is an art and demands an alert and active participation which seems to be beyond the capacity of many. Jesus apparently referred to this when he said, "Hearing they hear not" (Matt. 13:13).

To become adept at this art requires effort. Learning to listen must be undertaken with the same enthusiasm as learning music, painting, ballet, acting, or any of the art forms. In *The Art of Listening*, Dominick A. Barbara[1] indicates that learning the art of listening requires at least three things.

The art of listening requires discipline. Mastering this skill is complicated for the church leader because his normal training does not help. It may even be a hindrance. His training has prepared him to express himself, be convincing in his statements, forceably promote new schemes, and persuade people to accept responsibility in a church program. Now he must learn to curb all these impulses and become receptive and responsive. In many ways this is an about face and takes much self-discipline.

This art requires concentration. Most people have difficulty concentrating. They take a peculiar pride in doing a number of things at the same time. It has been said that we watch television and read and talk and eat and drink. A partially deaf man often went on trips in a car with a group of friends. He had a very efficient hearing aid and was able to enter freely into the conversation and communicate with the group. When he became tired or

40

bored, however, his simple technique was to switch off his hearing aid and take a nap. Though most people do not have a mechanical aid as did this man, many are similar to him in their listening habits. Listening is selective. Matthew Henry put it, "None so deaf as those that will not hear." It is imperative that the good listener become intellectually active and focus all of his hearing capacities upon the impressions which he receives.

Comprehension is important for effective listening. Comprehension is made difficult because most people think more rapidly than they speak. The rate of speech of most Americans is around 125 words a minute, but thought processes function at about four times this speed. Consequently, spare time is left for thinking. The use of this spare time often determines our effectiveness as listeners. As the speaker is expressing himself our thoughts turn to other things: what we had for breakfast, how we will balance the budget, or where we will spend our vacation. Every now and then we return to the speaker to catch up with him again. Then alas we dally too long over the delights of our future vacation and when we return we find the speaker has hopelessly outdistanced us and we finally give up the effort, and again we lapse into our own little dream world.

By way of contrast, the good listener is constantly following the speaker, seeking to extend and refine what is being said. This is particularly so in counseling, where the listener is actively seeking to evaluate the counselee's statements and comprehend the wider implications of what is being said.

Helpful Techniques in Listening

Shakespeare indicates that not listening is a disease. In the *Second Part of King Henry IV*, the Lord Chief Justice says to Falstaff, "You hear not what I say to you."

"Falstaff replies, "Very well, my lord, very well: . . . it is the disease of not listening, the malady of not marking, that I am troubled withal." [2] Consideration will now be given to the techniques which are helpful in the development of the art of listening, and careful attention to what follows may amount to a therapeutic experience which will help to cure the reader from the disease of "not listening."

Give the speaker your undivided attention.—Listening is not just a passive resignation to the inevitable in which the listener sinks into a dazed and benumbed condition. Nor is it a side activity to be engaged in while attending to more pressing and important matters.

Good listening requires that we project ourselves into another person's situation and try to understand a frame of reference which may be entirely different from our own. Such activity is not easy. One instruction given to counselors in a Western Electric Company was, "The interviewer should listen to the speaker in a patient and friendly, but intelligently critical manner." [3] The phrase "intelligently critical manner" indicates the necessary activity for good listening.

Marriage counselors are generally agreed that there are two types of complaints which come from married couples. Most men complain that their wives talk too much, and the wives that their husbands do not talk enough. In an article "Why Men Don't Talk to Their Wives," [4] the writer, incidentally a woman, claims that women do not pay enough attention to their husbands' conversations. She states that the conversation between two women is a mad race to see how much each can say before her opponent snatches the ball. Consequently, women have few scruples about interrupting their husbands.

This author claims that woolgathering is another check on a husband's conversation. In this process wives turn on the "beam and murmur" mechanism. While they nod fondly, they inwardly speculate as to next week's party, the new hat they saw in a shop, or the process of redecorating the bedroom. All of this, of course, is not confined to women.

A pastor noticed a female member of his church who was unusually popular. She always seemed to have a number of young men paying attention to her. One interview showed the reason— she looked intently at the speaker and grasped his every statement. She was a first-class listener.

Oliver dramatized this when he stated, "The listener leans towards it, his muscles taut, his eyes intent, his ears strained, his very breathing stopped." [5]

Interruption and woolgathering have no place in effective listening. There must be a scrupulous avoidance of the dazed look in the eye, the furtive glance at the watch, and the rearranging of desk top. The speaker must have the listener's undivided attention.

Do not display feelings of disapproval.—As people come for counseling, they sometimes have the wrong attitude. They may be belligerent, rude, or offensive. They might be telling obvious untruths or blatantly speaking about a breach of the moral code. The inward response of the leader to such statements is, of course, disapproval. If this becomes overt, he may rebuke the speaker and either stop or infuriate him. The church leader may have saved his own status but lost the opportunity to minister to this person.

Weatherhead suggests that the listener should not offer a rebuke. Though the speaker's statements are offensive, his coming to a religious leader about his trouble is an indication that he is aware of his shortcomings.

One can accept people without necessarily approving their behavior. The supreme example is that of our Lord Jesus Christ. In his ministry a woman taken in adultery was brought before him. He did not condemn the woman but accepted her as a person. Similarly, the church leader can accept people without necessarily giving the impression of approval of their conduct. This involves the previously stated expectation of nonretaliation. This is the right of anyone who comes for a conference with a counselor. One writer says that the general aim of a counseling interview is to provide a "zone of neutrality." Within this zone, a man at war with himself may even get to a permanent armistice.

Expression of hostility can, in itself, be a good sign. Carl Rogers has made much of this in his writings as he states that the more definite the negative feelings are that are expressed, the more certain it is that positive feelings and expressions will follow. This makes it necessary for the counselor to be patient and optimistic as to the ultimate outcome.

One of the keys to helping people by listening is the capacity to restrain one's self. Psychotherapist Wallen states, "We are fairly sure of one thing: criticising a patient for what he expresses tends to destroy his freedom to express himself." [6]

Develop helpful responses.—It has been seen that interrupting and showing disapproval cuts off the flow of conversation but, as important as this is, the opposite extreme must be guarded against. If the counselor sits like a bump on a log, it may be almost as bad; and the absence of response may seem to the speaker to reflect absence of interest. Appropriate responses are therefore very important.

Some authorities believe that the best responses in a counseling situation are short and contain within them an invitation to continue to talk. One writer claims that there are only four good listening responses—"Um," "Uh-huh," "Oh," and "I see." The best response has been described as "a series of eloquent grunts."

Response by manner can be helpful. Psychologists call this non-verbal communication. There are many stories of famous actors and speakers who have been able to convey almost as much by their gestures as by their speech. In counseling, nonverbal communication is very important, and it can take the form of a nod of the head, an understanding smile, or a gesture of the hand. With a little practice the would-be counselor can develop quite a skill in this type of communication.

Listen for the sound of silence.—Silence is important in listening. In his biography, Kaltenborn tells of his impressions as a student of the great William James. He describes an occasion when he was traveling with the great scholar. Looking around at the billboards and the blazing lights on every hand, he said it seemed as if they were living in a "megaphonic era." One wonders what William James would think of our day and age when radio and television keep constant both visual and auditory impressions.

Often people need to just get away. A troubled man told of going to a wise physician who sent him to spend a day at the beach. Here he was to remain in complete silence for the day. His first instruction was to listen carefully. Describing his experience, he mentioned remembering that "silence is the element in which great things fashion themselves." [7] The moment of silence can be the moment of revelation.

The counselor will learn to listen for the "sound of silence" and be prepared to let silence fall during the counseling conference. One counselor tells of spending periods up to five minutes in which not a word was spoken. Instead of feeling silence to be embarrassing, the church leader may see it as an effective tool in the counseling process.

When a silence becomes too long, it sometimes becomes necessary to break it. A good technique is to ask the person to elaborate on the point about which he was just speaking.

Creative Aspects of Listening

It has already been noted that listening is never a mere passivity nor is it just a psychological technique. One writer uses the phrase "creative listening" to describe the activity. Depicting the most significant of all creative acts for the Christian, medieval art often shows the conception of Jesus as being caused by the entrance of the Holy Spirit, usually in the form of a bird, into Mary's ear. In some of the more recent writings on the subject of religious doubt, much has been made of the importance of creative listening as a means of allowing expression and, consequently, growth in faith.

Listening can have significant spiritual values. "A word from the Eternal was rare in those days" (I Sam. 3:1, Moffatt). God needed someone to listen for what he had to say. Finally, the boy Samuel listened and heard the significant message that God was trying to communicate to his people. George Washington Carver, when asked the secret of his work, said, "I get up early in the morning and go out into the woods and listen for the voice of God." If we are prepared to listen, new worlds will open up for us; and it may be said of us, as it was of one a long time ago, "And thine ears shall hear a word behind thee, saying, This is the way, walk ye in it" (Isa. 30:21).

Part Two

The
Counseling
Process

IN THE FIRST section of this book an effort was made to give the layman psychological information and techniques which would help him in his normal informal relationships within the church.

This present section envisages the layman as becoming increasingly interested in counseling and sets about to take him into deeper aspects of the counseling process. A counseling relationship passes through fairly well-defined stages. A picture of the process all the way from the special opportunity facing the layman to the successful conclusion of a counseling experience is set forth.

Chapter 6 looks at the roots from which pastoral counseling has come and defines the term "pastoral" in this setting. It leads naturally to consideration of the peculiar situation of the church leader, some of the distinctives in his role, and the emphasis upon the "art" of counseling.

Chapter 7 discusses the matter of availability and considers the setting for the counseling relationship and the importance of appointments.

The exploratory encounter discussed in chapter 8 gives attention to the process of evaluation taking place in the minds of both the counselor and the counselee. The place of information in counseling and the difference between interviewing and counseling are dealt with.

No matter how gifted a counselor may be, he cannot help everybody who comes to him. There are many instances where he should get the person in touch with a more appropriate source of help. Making referrals is sometimes a very complex process. In chapter 9 some of the difficulties of referral are discussed, as well as the means of evaluating appropriate sources of assistance.

As counseling involves a peculiar relationship, it is essential that it should be entered into with great care. Many who come for counseling have strange ideas as to what goes on, and one of the most meaningful things the counselor will do will be to make sure that the whole situation is properly structured. Chapter 10 looks into the matter of establishing the counseling relationship.

Oversimplification is always a temptation which besets the writer of a volume like this. Taking this risk, chapter 11 is set out as the heart of the counseling process. The motif of the book swells, as it were, to a crescendo in this chapter as an effort is made to show the supreme importance of the ministry of listening.

To know what we are really seeking to accomplish in counseling is not always easy. An important objective will always be to enable the counselee to gain insight into his difficulties. Some of the complexities of insight are discussed in chapter 12. From this discussion the chapter moves on to grapple with the problem of the best way to conclude the counseling relationship.

6. *The Unique Opportunity*

TODAY, because of the strain and tensions of the age in which we live, there is an ever increasing need for the services of the counselor, and an interest in counseling is becoming apparent in many areas of life. There are marriage counseling centers, child guidance clinics, family welfare bureaus, and numerous other counseling services of which our grandparents never dreamed. Since many people feel that their church leader is the one to whom they can turn when they need help, the church leader has suddenly discovered himself facing a unique opportunity.

This section of the book is an endeavor to show the educational director, the Sunday school teacher, and the other leaders of the church how they may recognize the need for counseling that exists within their church groups. An effort is then made to help these leaders develop the technical skills necessary so they may assist with the different types of personality problems they encounter. In order that the church leader might have a better perspective, a brief survey will first be made of the historical roots of the counseling movement as it is related to the church.

Some Historical Roots of Pastoral Counseling

The concept of counseling which is so widespread today is a comparatively modern idea. It is one of the responses of man to his fellow man as he sees his need. There are a number of roots from which this movement grew, but space will permit only a few of these. As will be seen by reading the Bible, some forms of counseling were carried on as early as the days of Moses. Throughout the history of the Christian church, there have always been great pastors and leaders who related themselves to their people and intuitively helped them.

As early as 1905, there was a developing interest within the church in uniting psychological and religious concepts. This is true of the Emmanuel Movement which resulted from the co-operation of two Episcopal clergymen and a doctor who produced the book *Religion and Medicine*.

In 1920 a well-educated church worker, Anton T. Boisen, was admitted to a mental hospital. After his recovery, he became the first chaplain in a public mental hospital. While there, he led a training course for theology students. From that came the idea of clinical pastoral education—actually working in a hospital under the guidance of a chaplain supervisor and in conjunction with doctors, nurses, social workers, and other members of the staff.

During World War II, many church leaders served in the army as chaplains. They frequently thought their work would, for the most part, consist of preaching and religious instruction. Later, they discovered that by far the greater portion of their time was spent counseling men who needed help.

From these and other influencing factors has come the recognition of the value of counseling, and most modern theological seminaries have departments which specialize in this field. The church leader is becoming more aware of the important role he plays in helping people with their emotional difficulties.

This larger role of the church leader is receiving greater recognition. Dr. Charles Kemp sent out a questionnaire to members of the American Psychological Association who were working as counselors on college and university campuses. Of the sixty-three people who responded to the questionnaire, only one rejected the idea that there was special need for a church worker to function as a counselor on college or university campuses. Many of those who responded went so far as to indicate that they thought such a counselor was absolutely essential. They qualified their remarks, however, by indicating that the religious counselor should not attempt to work in areas for which he is not prepared; he should be trained. As an academic standard, a master's degree in psychology was indicated. One of the most illuminating facts was Dr. Kemp's discovery that 65 per cent of the people who responded indicated they would be willing to make their files available to religious counselors.[1]

Pastoral Counseling

The term "pastoral counseling" is frequently used in church related counseling. Pastoral counseling describes not so much a person as an activity. The committee which reported on principles and terminology to the Southern Baptist Conference on Counseling and Guidance in 1958 suggested that, as descriptive adjectives in counseling, the words "pastoral," "Christian," and "religious" have about the same meaning. Each of these is used to designate counseling done in an explicitly Christian context.

The pastoral counseling and religious education movements have much in common and share an interest in psychology of religion, with its emphasis on the religious experience of individuals and groups. This is illustrated by the work of Dr. Karl R. Stolz, former dean of the Hartford School of Religious Education, who made significant contributions to the study of both psychology of religion and pastoral counseling. In many seminaries the responsibility for teaching pastoral counseling resides in the schools or departments of religious education.

Religious education has undergone a period of rapid development and the church staff today commonly includes such professionals as a minister of education, a youth worker, and various age-group workers. Working with these professional leaders are superintendents, teachers, and group leaders. These are the people who will be called upon in the rapidly expanding work of counseling.

The Peculiar Position of the Church Leader

Robert Felix, of the National Institute of Mental Health, says that 40 per cent of the people who seek help for their emotional problems turn first of all to their church leader. This person, a leader in some phase of the Christian community, has a position which makes him an obvious source of help when troubled people are looking for assistance with their problems. The unique position of the church leader stems from a number of facts which will be discussed in this section.

There are always people in the community who have an attitude of trustfulness and faith toward the church leader. From colonial days, when the minister was frequently the schoolmaster and trusted advisor of the community, the religious leader has occupied a symbolic position. In many instances he enjoys more confidence of the people than does any other professional person.

Another reason for the church leader's peculiar position is that he can take the initiative in calling on people. When he hears a whisper that a certain person needs help, he can act on the information and visit the home. Because of the practice of churches' encouraging their leaders to visit church members, such a visit will not seem at all strange. During the visit the church leader can sense whether or not difficulties really exist. No other professional person within the community can enter people's homes in this way without arousing some sort of suspicion.

The church leader is usually familiar with the total situation in which a person is placed. Since he generally knows the family background and the peculiar pressures being brought to bear upon the individual, he can more easily evaluate a developing emotional difficulty. He often has the information that a psychologist, psychiatrist, or social worker must obtain before an evaluation can be made.

If he has some psychological background, the church worker can often see emotional difficulties when they are in their initial state. As he is involved in the meetings of committees and other church organizations and watches activities taking place within the group, it will soon become obvious if a member behaves in a manner that suggests maladjustment. This puts him in a position to suggest that the individual seek help before the difficulty becomes too pronounced.

Another factor in the peculiar position of the religious leader is that he frequently is looked upon by the members of the group as being something of an authoritative figure. If a church member has misgivings about seeing a psychiatrist, the church leader often can allay his fears. He can deal with such rationalization as "I don't want to visit a psychiatrist because he would hurt my faith." Because he is within the religious community, people often will heed his words more readily than they would the advice of an outsider. In many small communities the church leader is frequently one of the best educated persons and one of the few people with any knowledge of mental health. Therefore, a heavy responsibility for the mental health of the citizenry rests upon his shoulders.

Distinctives in Counseling in a Church Setting

There are a number of distinctives in the work of the religious counselor. This church worker never must forget he is first and foremost a leader of a religious group and that the people who come to him see him as such. Because of the nature of his work and the many demands which are made on him, he will not have a highly specialized counselor's training. Consequently, the work which he can do effectively will be limited.

The church leader does not have a professional setting within which to work, but functions within the organization of the church. It follows that it is not possible for him to select the people with whom he will counsel, as a professional counselor can. If he discriminates between counselees and it becomes obvious, he will create difficulties within the group. An example of this is the young man who was working with a group of students in a church student center. It was not very long before some of the less attractive girls discovered that though he had little time to discuss their problems, he always found time for a conference with the attractive campus queen. The group soon lost confidence in this man's ministry.

Another distinctive of counseling within a church setting is that the church leader is "enduringly related" to the members of his group. Mrs. Jones, a prominent member in the church, came one day to talk with her pastor. He could see that she was anxious and overencouraged her to talk. Though reluctant, she at last told her suspicions of her husband, a deacon in the church, and a young widow who lived nearby. When later she and her husband were reconciled, her pastor was a threat to her; for he alone knew the situation which had existed. She, therefore, became a thorn in his side and constantly rallied opposition to his ministry. Finally, the minister had to leave the church. Such a situation would never have arisen had he been a counselor in a professional setting, but because he was enduringly related to the group, the pastor's counseling brought about this complication.

A leader within a church organization sometimes discovers that helping people with marital problems may have a disappointing sequel. After inconveniencing himself to help them, he feels disillusioned when, having patched up their differences, they leave his organization and go off to join another church. Once again the problem is that he knows too much about them and they feel he is a threat. Some professional counselors make it a point never to meet their counselees outside of a counseling session. The nature of his relationship prevents the church leader from following this policy.

A church leader may become too interested in counseling. There is always the possibility that he may imagine he is an amateur psychiatrist and, from this, feel he has a special prestige. He can become obsessed with the idea of hearing other people's confidences and exploring their lives. Sometimes, this may go as far as to cause him to enter vicariously into other people's experiences. Moreover, if the work which he is doing within a church situation is not very successful, he may tend to concentrate on the ministry of counseling; this may become an escape from a ministry of mediocrity.

The Art of Counseling

The church leader is engaged in a counseling ministry of a special type. It is what Bonnell calls "spiritual therapy." Because this is termed spiritual therapy, it does not mean that it will be accomplished by the techniques which are generally utilized in religious work. Counseling is different from the preaching ministry in which the preacher makes his dogmatic declarations. Neither is it a promotional ministry in which the church leader endeavors to rally support for his program. In preaching or promoting there is a one-way verbal communication. The leader speaks and the group listens. Any response from the group is nonverbal in nature. In counseling, however, there is a two-way communication, and the counselee talks more than the counselor.

Counseling is not so much a science as an art. Though counseling theories and techniques are the products of research and experimentation, they are readily abandoned when the counselor intuitively feels that another approach would be more profitable. The objective pose of the scientist is replaced by the subjective response of the sensitive personality.

Counseling is an educational procedure and, as such, has much in common with good teaching techniques. Brayfield, an authority in the field of counseling, suggests that the counselor remember that there are five elements which are important in both teaching and counseling. These are:

(1) We do not learn if we are emotionally blocked or if our mind is distracted by personal problems that take our attention away from the classroom. (2) We do not learn if the ideas or vocabulary of the teacher are over our head. (3) We do not learn if too many ideas or facts are thrown at us at one time. (4) Most important, we do not learn if we are given no opportunity to participate in the learning experience. (5) We do not learn if the halting expressions of our deep feelings and attitudes are received with scorn, a casual bit of reassurance, obvious embarrassment, or other attitudes which hinder our expression.[2]

It is now possible to make a definition of counseling. One of the greatest authorities in the field is Carl Rogers, who has been greatly influenced by educational concepts. Dr. Rogers defines counseling thus: "Effective counseling consists of a definitely structured, permissive relationship which allows the client to gain an understanding of himself to a degree which enables him to take positive steps in the light of his new orientation." [3] It will be noted that in this definition there is much stress upon the counselee. This has led Rogers to speak of his type of counseling as "client-centered therapy." This emphasis on the individual is in keeping with the Christian tradition and will be followed in the consideration of counseling in this book.

There are several qualifications that are essential for any person who is to be a counselor. Rogers has given a clear setting out of these in his book *Counseling and Psychotherapy*, and these will be followed in this section. These qualifications include:

A sensitivity to human relationships.—This is hard to define, but it means the capacity to feel the reaction of other people, to understand how they are responding, and to sense the bond which comes to be established between the counselor and the counselee.

Objectivity.—The counselor must have the ability to stand off and look at the situation, to be understanding and yet not become too involved in the relationship.

Respect for the individual.—This is a belief that the person has growth capacity. Accordingly, the counselor will not attempt to dominate the counselee.

An understanding of self.—An effective counselor must know something of the workings of his own personality, his limitations, and shortcomings. He must also have some insight into his own peculiar neurotic reactions. If he does not understand this, he may be warped and biased in his judgment when seeking to evaluate other people's emotions.

Psychological knowledge.—The counselor should have as much knowledge in this field as possible. A good background in general psychology helps, as does a knowledge of the theories of personality, psychological testing, and at least an introduction to abnormal psychology.

It was previously noted that counseling is an art. If this is true, it is an art that can be learned. It has been said: "Teachers are born, not made, but they are not born made." The same is true of counselors. There are many who have the gift, but few are so proficient that they could not profit by further training. The church leader who has an interest in counseling should take fresh courage as he prepares for his task. If he really feels for people, respects their personal integrity, understands something about himself, he can by study, training, and practice develop skills that will enable him to help people in a counseling relationship.

7. Availability for Contact

IF THE CHURCH leader is to counsel effectively, he must be available and people must know of his availability. Moreover, there must be a system enabling the person needing help to contact the church leader.

One of the difficulties the church leader faces as he launches his counseling ministry is that of letting people know that he is available to help them. The stereotype in which most people place a church leader is that of a man hurrying madly from one place to another. He constantly overworks himself, will not stop to take a rest, and is always on the verge of a collapse because of the abandon with which he throws himself into his work. National magazines thunder warnings that ministers are breaking down.

"I am too busy" to rest or to socialize is often heard from the lips of people in positions of church leadership. Such activity is often very commendable. In many ways it is very satisfying to feel there are people who are willing to expend themselves so freely in a great cause. However, it must be admitted that the church worker is not as busy as he appears to be.

Ordway Tead, in his book *The Art of Leadership*,[1] speaks of the importance of the leader dramatizing his energy. He says that whenever the leader appears before his group, he ought to appear full of vitality and vigor. He should not be lethargic nor give the impression of tiredness. Such a concept is commendable, but the advantage of creating such an image in the minds of his followers may be offset by the fact that he seems to them to be unapproachable. The church leader often has the experience of being apologetically approached with, "I know you are terribly busy and that I have no right to take your time." Hulme suggests the church leader needs to take cognizance of this and says, "Busyness . . . is one of the most acceptable escape mechanisms of our day." [2]

Making Availability Known

The church leader who desires to counsel needs to let it be known that he is available. He can sometimes do this obliquely in one of his talks or announcements by referring to his pleasure in the opportunity of talking with a member of his group. If there is a class publication, he can announce in it when he will be available for conferences.

A rather unusual arrangement is quoted by Russell Dicks in *Pastoral Work and Personal Counseling*.[3] He tells of a pastor who sent out cards to the young people of his church to let them know that he would be available at a specific time if they cared to come by and talk with him. He says that at first this arrangement was somewhat formal and those who came were not too much at ease. However, on the second visit, they began to feel more at ease and to discuss their problems more freely.

Informal Contacts

In a discussion of the people who help others in their difficulties, Skidmore, Garret, and Skidmore make an unusual evaluation of the nurse: "In the hospital setting the nurse gets acquainted with the patient on a personal basis, and because of this many of the ordinary social barriers are removed. The patient is likely to "bare his soul" to her for a 'psychological bath' at times." [4] People accidentally thrown together often establish easy and helpful relationships. This is what Oates calls the "market place ministry."

In chapter 3 a more detailed examination was made of informal contacts. It is sufficient here to note that this is one of the most important aspects of availability. Seeking to help a teacher prepare his lesson, a Sunday school superintendent may find a great opportunity to help that teacher prepare himself for a crisis in his interpersonal relationships.

A Suitable Setting

As good as informal counseling can be, it is frequently only a starting point for a more meaningful relationship. An effective counseling relationship cannot be established if there is a group of teen-agers yelling and shouting in the background. Moreover, the church leader is usually much in demand at these informal gatherings, and interruptions are therefore frequent. It is often best to use this casual encounter as a starting place and to suggest that the individual drop by the church office at a convenient time.

The church leader should try to provide a good setting for a counseling conference. If he is a Sunday school teacher, it might be advisable for him to see if he can get the use of one of the church offices. The most important feature of an office for counseling is that it should be private. There is a psychological value when two people talk in feeling that everything else is at least temporarily excluded. Therefore, it is beneficial either to have no telephone or to have one with a cut-off key. However, while this office should be private, it is preferable for it to be located in a public or semipublic setting. In all probability, the best meeting place will be at the church where there are other people.

The type of furniture which is used in the office is not of great importance. The office should be furnished with a desk and a couple of chairs. Drapes and well chosen pictures will help. Some secular counselors are now saying that the counseling room is better without the desk. There are two reasons for this. One is that the counselor, who is sitting behind the desk, looks too authoritative. It is also claimed by some counselors that a desk causes a barrier between counselor and counselee. However, in a church situation, the chair behind the desk is probably the best arrangement.

The counselee should not have to sit in some place where light, either from the lamp or the window, will cause him discomfort. One counselor noticed that his counselee constantly squinted, and he wondered if this were a nervous manifestation. Later, he discovered that her eyes were sensitive to light, and all that was needed was an adjustment of the window shade.

A package of Kleenex is always useful in a counseling room and a private exit helps in allowing the disturbed counselee to slip away without being observed.

The Importance of Appointments

Some type of an appointment system is of value, if not an absolute necessity, if a counseling situation is to continue for more than one session. An appointment system helps to save the counselor from becoming involved in counseling procedure in inappropriate spots. For example, members of the family or friends may be present when a church leader visits one of his group. If the member begins to tell of some problem that is worrying him, it is generally preferable for the leader to suggest a time for a conference in the privacy of a church office.

There are psychological benefits in making an appointment. It is a very personal arrangement, and it helps the counselee to feel that the counseling hour is his. The church leader, whom he perceives as a busy person, has taken time out and has said, in effect, that he will set aside thirty minutes of his time to focus all of his attention upon the counselee. This is the counselee's moment. The personal element in the arrangement helps to make for a good counseling relationship.

Having to take the initiative in making an appointment may give impetus to the counseling relationship. According to Rogers, the first characteristic step in the counseling process is that the individual comes for help. He says that "rightly recognized, this is one of the most significant steps in therapy." [5] Confirmation of this theory comes from a number of sources. One of these is the experience of Alcoholics Anonymous. Clinebell says, "AA rightly recognizes that an alcoholic's own desire for sobriety is an indispensable ingredient in any plan of help." [6] The amazing success that this organization has had with alcoholics is due, in part at least, to their insistence that the alcoholic must have a keen desire to break with his habit. The church leader labors at a disadvantage when asked by fond parents or enthusiastic friends to approach a person whom they consider to be in need of help.

From the beginning the odds are against this counseling situation because the prospective counselee did not take the initiative.

Some counselors claim that even if an appointment is cancelled, the step taken has value for the person involved. Confirmation of this came from the report of Robert L. Faucet at the annual meeting of the National Council on Family Relations, in 1955. Dr. Faucet described a study of people who had made appointments but had not kept them. Six months later responses to a questionnaire reflected that 50 per cent of them were getting along satisfactorily and needed no help. Dr. Faucet concluded that the process of making up one's mind to get help and actually making contact with a person or agency for help serves as a dynamic in the problem-solving process. The appointment, then, serves as a check-point and may precipitate an evaluation which helps in adjustment.

The person who makes an appointment must make a certain investment of time. Church leaders often worry about this, feeling that it places a burden upon the person making the appointment. However, in many areas of counseling, emphasis is placed upon the necessity of the counselee's making a contribution to the counseling process. Some psychologists will not counsel if a fee is not paid. They do this, not just to get the money, but because psychologically it is important that the counselee make some investment in the process. In at least one marriage counseling center, the indigent person is counseled but is required to work around the center to pay the fee. The church leader is in a position where he cannot ask fees for counseling, as this would disrupt the peculiar relationship which he has with people in the work of the church. But he can give an impetus to the counseling situation by asking counselees to make an investment of their time.

Sometimes a broken appointment may cause embarrassment to both counselor and counselee. Because of this, the counselee may feel that there is a barrier which prevents his return to the counselor. The mature counselor will write a note saying that he missed the counselee and suggest a time for another appointment, thus opening the way for a renewed relationship.

Summary

Availability is very important. He who hopes to counsel must give people the impression that he is willing to accept them and that he is anxious to be of assistance. Whether by announcement, personal contact, or general attitude, it is of vital importance that the church leader acquaint the members of the group with his availability. He must also provide a setting for the counseling encounter and institute some mechanics which will help to bring him together with his counselee. Informal contacts sometimes result in accidental precounseling encounters which may lead to more meaningful counseling experiences. An appointment system is more than an administrative device, for it has many psychological values for the counselee.

8. *The Exploratory Encounter*

WHEN COUNSELEE and counselor meet for the first time, a process of evaluation begins in both minds. The prospective counselee attempts to evaluate the counselor and seeks to discover how far he can trust him. He may have worried or tried hard for a long time to find enough courage to even talk to a counselor. Now he is filled with misgivings, wondering whether or not he should have come to such a person.

Sometimes after just one interview the counselee will feel that he has found the solution to his problem. The competent counselor will take this at face value and let the counselee depart if he so desires. However, by some neutrally toned conversation, he may be able to win the confidence of the counselee so that a counseling relationship can begin.

Gaining Rapport

Establishing a good counseling relationship is called rapport. English and English define rapport as "a comfortable and unconstrained relationship of mutual confidence between two or more persons." [1]

Rapport is facilitated by a number of factors. The first is the ability of the counselor to make his warmth and sincerity apparent. This does not mean that he becomes effusive with enthusiastic greetings, as this may cause the counselee to call up his latent sales resistance. The counselor should lead the counselee to feel that he is genuinely interested in him and that he accepts him as a person.

John Charles Wynn warns against a number of booby traps for

counselors. One of these he calls the "see-here-you-poor-soul-pose." [2] Such a condescending air will not help in establishing a good counseling relationship. Earlier it was noted that many professionals have removed their desks from the counseling rooms. One of the strongest arguments in favor of this is that if the counselor sits behind his desk, he looks too much like a figure of authority. The idea is that the counselee must come to understand that he is accepted as a person, not as an inferior.

Another factor in establishing rapport is the assurance that everything that happens in this relationship will be kept confidential. Something can be learned from the confessional of the Roman Catholic Church and the confidence which its members place in their priests. It may be necessary at times to assure the counselee that everything said in the counseling session will be kept confidential. The leader must be very careful to make sure this is so. The church leader will often be elated by his counseling experiences and may be tempted to recount them to his fellow workers. This is one of the traps to be avoided.

Another important factor in gaining rapport is the capacity of the counselor to listen. Free, unguided talk is important at all times but is doubly important at the beginning. As the counselee tells his story, he feels the counselor is an *insider* and is more comfortable with him. The willingness of the counselor to sit and listen builds his feeling of good will. An illustration of this may be found in Dale Carnegie's book *How to Win Friends and Influence People*. In one chapter, "An Easy Way to Become a Good Conversationalist," he tells of going to a party where a celebrated botanist was guest of honor. Carnegie asked questions which launched the famous man into a conversation which lasted throughout the evening. When it was time to go, the botanist told his host that Carnegie was "a most interesting conversationalist," although Carnegie had hardly spoken a word. He tells his secret: "I had listened intently. I had listened because I was genuinely interested." [3] Carnegie concludes: "Be a good listener. Encourage others to talk about themselves." [4] The counselor has a different purpose, but a similar process takes place as he listens.

In the development of rapport an important factor is that the counselor is not a part of the counselee's inner life. While in some ways the counselee sees the counselor as quite close to him, in other respects he sees him at a distance. He is outside his circle of friends, acquaintances, and relatives. The counselee can discuss things freely, feeling that the counselor, while warm and accepting, is not close enough to know him or his friends on a personal basis; therefore, he can safely reveal himself.

Rapport is the beginning of a relationship which is important in any aspect of counseling but is particularly so in a religious setting. For, as Belgum says, "Relationships are a fundamental concern of Christianity." [5] The counseling relationship is described by Mudd: " 'Relationship' as used here refers to the interaction between counselor and counselee, which becomes a motivating force in the changes and growth which take place in the counseling procedure." [6] As the counseling process continues, the developing relationship will become increasingly significant and will require careful control by the counselor.

Assessing the Counselee

As the counselee tries to evaluate the counselor, a similar process takes place in the mind of the counselor. The counselor tries to discover the degree of the problem. The beginning counselor is sometimes surprised to find that the problem first presented is not the *real* problem, but often this is not soon revealed.

Because the counseling session takes place within a church, there will be a tendency for the original problem to be either a religious matter or something to do with the organization of the church. It does not necessarily mean that the problem *is* religious. One minister told of a man who said he would become a Christian if the preacher could show him where Cain got his wife. After a long talk, it turned out that it was not Cain's wife who was worrying him, but somebody else's wife. Very often it will be discovered that after the facade of religious perplexity has been demolished, the more personal and emotionalized issues become the focus of attention.

It is apparently less threatening to discuss theological issues than to face one's personal maladjustments. Particular attention needs to be paid to this point when dealing with students. Most of their problems are emotional rather than intellectual.

A speaker at a function near a college campus was approached by a student who requested a conference. During the course of the conference, the student told of his difficulties in accepting the conservative view of the authorship of the Pentateuch. The visitor began immediately to present the conservative point of view. When he finally finished, the student thanked him and started to leave. As he reached the doorway, the student again thanked the visitor and said, "By the way, while I was out in my automobile with a girl the other evening. . . ." Out tumbled a story of guilt and self-recrimination. The discussion of the Pentateuch was wasted because the counselor had not given his counselee enough time to express himself.

In these situations, the perceptive counselor accepts the problem presented but does not become too deeply immersed in it until he is sure it is the *real* problem. He keeps an open mind in the early stages of the counseling relationship and remains alert for any turn the presentation may take.

In informal encounters, the church leader sometimes finds that a person merely needs information. Books are written in so many specialized areas that there likely will be at least one dealing with the particular case. Because of the great number of books available, the church leader should know a volume before he recommends it. The following standards can assist the church leader in his selection:

(1) What the reviewers say. Watch for reviews in reputable publications.

(2) Consult your local librarian. This man is an expert in his field and may be able to give an objective evaluation.

(3) Beware of cure-all literature. Some writers oversimplify life and offer such widespreading solutions that they only cause further confusion.

(4) Does the author lead you to other sources of help? A good writer leads the reader to the people from whom he has learned. One

of the chief values of a stimulating book is that it leads you to other relevant literature.

(5) Does the author give you some humor, encouragement, and hope along the way? Some books are so analytical and negative that they bring little help, serving only to confuse and alarm.

(6) Is the author a recognized authority on the subject? It may be his first book and contain immature concepts. Find out something about him.

(7) Is the book publisher reputable? There are various kinds of publishers. Learn if this one is reputable.

(8) For whom was the book written? Was it written for the person to whom you are planning to lend it? Some books are technical and if you have been studying in the field, it may suit you, but it may not be suitable for the one to whom you are planning to lend it.[7]

Some counselors have a "loan shelf" containing the types of books that will help people: literature on youth problems, sex, love, marriage, vocational information, etc. A list of these books will be found in the Appendix.

In *Man and Wife,* Mudd makes the point that a counselee may feel all he wants is information, but in reality this is not so. She states:

Realization by the client that the opportunity to talk out the way he feels about things with a receptive, sympathetic, and realistically oriented counselor is probably more important to him than covering any prescribed amount of information.[8]

It is probably best for the counselor to withhold this type of information to make sure that the counselee has had an opportunity to express himself and to discover that information is really needed.

Interviewing and Counseling

Wayne Oates makes a sensible differentiation between counseling and interviewing. He states that interviewing usually involves only one contact; whereas, in counseling there is more than one meeting on a planned basis. Interviewing concentrates on the quick solution of an immediate problem that is irritating the individual. Counseling depends upon a more leisurely development of the relationship. Such a relationship aims at the achievement of insight as well as the spiritual and emotional growth of the counselee. While this distinction is not made in most of the literature, it is helpful in this discussion. Following is a suggested outline of the process of interviewing:

(1) The interviewer has an understanding with his interviewee about how much time they have at their disposal.

(2) Two thirds of the time is spent in listening to the person present his problem.

(3) The interviewer then sets about filling in the gaps of missing information by asking pertinent questions.

(4) The fourth step is to discover how the person attempted to solve the problem before he came to the church leader.

(5) The church leader should now set about to try to explore the possible alternatives of action which the person may take.

(6) The sixth step is to try to predict with the person the possible outcomes that the alternative powers of action might have.

(7) Finally the church leader can leave the decisions as to action to be taken in the counselor's hands.[9]

Most of the contacts of the church leader will fall into the above category. The American Institute of Family Relations, in Los Angeles, California, has estimated that 25 per cent of the people who come to seek help come for just one visit. From this, it is apparent that a single interview can help.

Seward Hiltner indicates that "brief counseling" can perform at least three functions:

It can help the parishioner to "turn the corner" with reference to the situation. By discussing the matter with the church leader, the counselee is better able to clarify his position and to prepare the way for a decision.

It can constitute "supportive counseling." A person may have experienced a terrible shock. Momentarily, it seems as if his world is shattered. It is not a matter of seeing through a neurosis or the subtle factors involved in a psychological defense, but the need of the counselee to feel there is someone who is concerned. The church leader stands by and supports the counselee through the crisis.

Brief counseling "can do no harm." If it does not help, it will probably not hinder and there is always the possibility that help will come from such an experience. Consequently, it is important for the church leader to see these brief encounters as helpful, even if they do not develop into a full, formal counseling experience.[10]

One writer, speaking of the voyage of Christopher Columbus, said, "When he started out, he didn't know where he was going, when he arrived he didn't know where he was, and when he returned he didn't know where he had been, but he discovered America." Similarly, in some of his counseling experiences, the church leader will feel that he is something of a Columbus during this exploratory encounter. However, let him take fresh courage and remember that in the wonder of interpersonal relationships he is often being much more helpful than he ever dreamed he could be.

9. Making Referrals

THE CHURCH leader does not have the training, ability, or experience to help every counselee who comes to him. Moreover, he should not attempt to work in areas where another is more qualified to help. Getting counselees in touch with suitable assistance is called referral. Referral is not easy, for to use this device successfully, one must have tact, skill, and patience.

The process of referral begins when, after due consideration of all aspects of the counselee's problem, the counselor realizes that this case is beyond him. The counselor tells the counselee of his inadequacy in this area and suggests someone else who can be of greater help to him. At this moment the counselee may feel that he is being rejected by the church leader, whom he sees as trying to pass him off to someone else, or he may become unduly optimistic about the outcome of the anticipated contact. It is necessary for the counselor to tread warily between these two pitfalls by giving assurances of continued interest on the one hand and realistically presenting the possibilities of assistance on the other.

Referrals Within the Church

A modern church is often a complex organization and may have as many as five or six professionals who function at different age levels. These staff members may be helpful with difficulties in specific areas. Also, there may be schoolteachers, physicians, psychologists, social workers and other competent people willing to help their fellow church members. The church leader can help to make arrangements for consultation with one of these.

The pastor will always be an important figure in referral. Referral is sometimes called a "two-way street," meaning that social workers or psychiatrists not only see people sent by the pastor but also send people to see their minister. In interchurch relationships, referral will also be a two-way street in another way. Without encumbering him with trivialities, the good church leader sees that his pastor is familiar with information vital for his effective pastoral work. The busy minister is sometimes ignorant about what is going on in the grass roots of church life. Even information about illness and death is frequently not sent to the pastor early enough. It is small wonder that the pastor is often unaware of the more intimate personal problems. By acquainting the pastor with these problems, the layman renders a fine service. A church leader is seen fulfilling this responsibility in the following incident. The WMU president comes to the pastor's office:

Pastor: Come in, Mrs. Greenway. How is the WMU?

Mrs. Greenway: (smiling) Well, I guess the organization is doing well, but right now I am concerned about one of our members. I was helping Mrs. Green put on her choir robe and she began to cry. She told me her husband left home last night and said he was not coming back again. Just at that moment another choir member came in and our conversation was cut off. I haven't had a chance to see her again so I thought I would let you know.

Pastor: Thank you for telling me. I'll make it my business to call on her.

The church leader's help in sighting such evidence of trouble is of vital importance to the pastor.

More specifically, in the generally accepted sense of the word, effective referral work can be done by the church leader. The following conversation shows a Sunday school teacher in action:

Mr. Murray: I'm sorry about missing Sunday school so much, but I just don't like to go without Sue, and she refuses to come with me.

Mr. Barnard: You feel embarrassed about coming by yourself?

Mr. Murray: Yes, I do. Sue and I hardly ever seem to do anything together these days. I don't know what to do about it. We really need some sort of help, but I wouldn't know where to go.

Mr. Barnard: Have you ever thought of talking to the pastor?

Mr. Murray: I did want to, but he is so busy and I wouldn't want to waste his time.

Mr. Barnard: I think you will find that Rev. James thinks that counseling is one of the most valuable things that he does. Why don't you call up and make an appointment to see him?

Mr. Murray: I think I'll do that.

The Sunday school teacher has brought a ray of hope to Mr. Murray. He has corrected the false idea of the pastor's priorities. However, he has left the iniative in Mr. Murray's hands, giving him the feeling that the interview is his own arrangement. A judicious word to the pastor can pave the way for an effective referral.

Social Service Agencies

Kemp says that there have been three stages in the relationship of the church to social service. During the first period, the church did almost all of it; later there came a separation, and now there is a trend toward co-operation. This trend is coming from both the churches and the social service agencies.

One survey shows that a large percentage of people turn to their church in time of trouble. While this is fine, it may happen that their church will not know what to tell them. At a recent gathering a group of ministers revealed that they knew very little about their community's social agencies. It is possible that the church leader knows even less. To remedy the situation, both the ministers and the church leaders should familiarize themselves with the social-service resources within the community. These differ within communities, but most cities have some type of directory of social service agencies which will prove a veritable gold mine for the church leader. If there is no directory, such information can be put on cards and kept in the church office for reference.

To develop a knowledge of community resources, Dr. Kemp has suggested that the church worker find the answers to the following questions:

Where do you go if a man wants a job?

Where do you go if a transient wants a meal and a room for the night?

Where do you go for help for an alcoholic?

Where do you go when parents wonder if their child is retarded?

Where do you go if a husband and wife are having difficulty and it seems to be a deeper problem than the pastor feels adequate to handle?

Where do you go if a family does not have sufficient clothing to send a child to school?

Where do you go if there is an older person who needs nursing-home care but does not have the funds to provide it?

Where do you go if a boy wants to study for the ministry but isn't sure whether or not he has the intellectual capacity to finish college?

Where do you go to find help or a foster home for a neglected child?

Where do you go to find help for a family that needs legal assistance but cannot afford to hire an attorney?

How do you find out if a person or a family has been consulting other agencies?[1]

A church leader with an interest in this sort of work should purchase *The Pastor and Community Resources*, by Charles F. Kemp, published by the Bethany Press. In the latter part of this book is not only a complete index of the national headquarters of social service agencies but also space for entering the names, addresses, and telephone numbers of local agencies.

In some situations, knowledge of facilities available in nearby communities is valuable. The following encounter shows where this information helped:

Mr. Harris: It's nice of you to call on me about the Brotherhood meeting. I surely used to enjoy getting together with those men at the church.

Mr. Moore: We really would like to have you come to our next meeting. It is ladies' night. Bring your wife along with you. You will both enjoy it.

Mr. Harris: Well, that's part of the problem. Things are not going so well with Jean and me.

Mr. Moore: Have you ever thought about talking to Dr. Summers about it? He does a lot of counseling.

Mr. Harris: Well, it's a strange thing. We both think the world of Dr. Summers. He has always been so nice to us; in fact, that's the problem. I would hate for him to know about us. I don't think

anyone suspects anything, and we had rather not go to Dr. Summers. If there were only someone else.

Mr. Moore: Have you heard about the Marriage and Counseling
Center at Jester? That's twenty miles away and you wouldn't
be known. I'd be happy to give you the address if you would like
it.

Mr. Harris: Thanks.

This is not an unusual situation. People are often very anxious to
maintain their status in the eyes of their minister. We have previously noted that sometimes a couple who has been counseled
because of martial difficulties will leave the church after the
minister has gone to a lot of trouble to help them. In some places
ministers refer church members to other pastors in the town in the
belief that their relationship to this particular couple will hinder
counseling. Here is an area where the church leader can render a
special service by making available information about nearby
social service facilities.

A morning spent in visiting social service agencies will enable
the church leader to become familiar with the objectives and key
personnel of the various organizations. This will facilitate later
referrals.

Making contact with the agency will probably be the responsibility of the church leader. A telephone call may be sufficient.
Sometimes a letter is called for, and on other occasions the counselee may need assistance with the agency's intake procedures. In
this latter case, it may be necessary for the church leader to ac-
company his counselee to the agency and see that he gets started
successfully.

Referrals for Psychological Help

There are many strange motivations at work in emotional illness, and these sometimes cause the sick person to turn to the
fellowship of the church. Oates' investigations showed that there
were always a number of people who turned to religion as a "last
straw" in an effort to cope with unmanageable personal problems.
Some of these are so serious that the church leader can do little to

help. If there is any doubt in the leader's mind about the serious-
ness of an emotional disturbance in a given case, he should waste
no time in getting a professional evaluation. In *The Clergyman's
Guide to Recognizing Mental Illness*, Klink gives ten simple
criteria to guide in detecting a serious mental disturbance.

(1) He shows big changes in his behavior.
(2) He has strange periods of confusion or loss of memory.
(3) He thinks people are plotting against him or he has grandiose
ideas about himself.
(4) He talks to himself and hears voices.
(5) He thinks people are watching him or talking about him.
(6) He sees visions or smells strange odors or has peculiar tastes.
(1) He has complaints of bodily changes that are not possible.
(8) He suffers from the need to perform several repetitive acts
many times over or is plagued by foreboding thoughts.
(9) He shows marked depressed behavior.
(10) He behaves in a way that is dangerous to others.[2]

These are only guides and, in their milder forms, are seen in most
normal people. When they are observed in their exaggerated
manifestations, the counselor should move to get professional help
for his counselee.

Selecting a Trustworthy Counselor

In these days there are many people who set themselves up as
counselors. The church leader obviously will not send his counselee to Sister Anna who specializes in readings and advice, but he
may have difficulty in deciding upon the merits of a professional
person. Oates comes to our aid by suggesting criteria by which
an evaluation can be made.[3] A selection of these will be used in
this consideration.

Who sponsors your counselor?—If the counselor is sponsored
by some reputable agency, there will be much more reason to accept him than if the agency does not have a high standing in the
community.

Has the person been in the community very long?—The longer
a person has been in a community the more reason there will be

to believe that he has stood the test of time in his work. If he is a
new arrival, he may have yet to prove himself.

Has the person been adequately trained for his task?—The psychiatrist will be an M.D. who has had specialized training over
and above his normal medical training. The psychoanalyst is generally an M.D. who has had specialized training in Freudian psychology. His training includes being psychoanalyzed and using
Freudian techniques. The clinical psychologist generally has a
Ph.D. in psychology with a special clinical internship. The social
worker has done graduate work in a school of social work. With
marriage counselors it is not so easy to make an evaluation. However, an adequate graduate degree is a bare minimum for these
people.

*Has the counselor been reasonably successful in dealing with
other people's problems?*—There is always a pragmatic test which
may be applied to a counselor's work. It is reasonable to expect
that he should have had a certain amount of success in helping
other people.

*Does this person promise much and do little, or does he promise
little and do much?*—The church leader should always be careful
of the person who is constantly boasting about his tremendous
successes, for this very often may be but a cover-up for his
inherent sense of inferiority.

Is the counselor a person of basic spiritual integrity?—There are
some people who have very adequate technical training and yet
have no respect for spiritual values. This is always a note of concern for the religious worker as he makes referrals. Because he *is*
a worker in a church he needs to be reasonably sure that the counselee will not feel that the professional has a purely pagan approach to life.

A referral to a psychiatrist, child guidance clinic, or clinical
psychologist must be handled very carefully. The church leader
will often have to interpret the function of the professional to the
counselee. Many people are very sensitive to the word psychologist or psychiatrist. A jesting reference to "head shrinkers" by
the counselee may reveal an underlying anxiety. "Emotional ill-

ness" is a good term that can be used tactfully in these interpretations.

The family's help may have to be enlisted, and a tactful approach is vital. Very often the pastor can help and should be invited to do so. The sympathetic physician will be invaluable in these delicate procedures.

Making Contact

Referrals to psychologists or psychiatrists may have to be handled in a more formal manner than those to social service agencies. Sometimes the counselor can make the appointment; however, it is generally best for the counselee to make his own appointment. This gives him a feeling that it belongs to him and he must accept the responsibility for it.

It is helpful if, before the first interview, the church leader will take time to write a letter to the professional, giving background information. A good referral letter should tell how the counselee came to the counselor's attention; a concise description of the number and nature of the conversations which the counselor has had with the counselee; a description of his problem, insofar as possible in the same words that the counselee used himself; and a statement of the facts known to the counselor about the history of the counselee.[4]

If the referral is being made to a psychiatrist, psychiatric and psychological jargon should be avoided as far as possible. Such a letter might read:

Dr. Blanchard
Medical Arts Building
Fort Worth, Texas

Dear Dr. Blanchard:

I understand that Mrs. Dennis has an appointment to see you on Thursday of next week. In the belief that she is in need of the sort of professional evaluation and aid which you can give, I suggested that she visit you.

Mrs. Dennis is a teacher in the Adult I department of our Sunday school where I am superintendent. She teaches a group of young married women. For some time now, members of her class have been telling of strange things she has been saying and doing.

She is forty-seven years of age and has a family of five children—three girls and two boys. Her husband is a mailman who seems to be a conscientious bread winner, but he does not share many of her interests. Two of Mrs. Dennis' children are happily married, but one of the daughters is having a considerable amount of domestic trouble. Mrs. Dennis often expresses concern about this.

I talked some with Mrs. Dennis, and she has mentioned, "The neighbors across the street are sending rays into my body." She also mentioned that she felt that some of the younger women in her Sunday school class were apparently trying to lure her husband away from her. There seems to be no factual basis for this assertion.

The onset of this condition has been gradual. It was about six months ago that some of these attitudes began to be obvious.

If there is anything that I can do to help in this situation, I will be happy to co-operate in any way that I can.

Sincerely yours,

BILL JONES

A Continuing Ministry

A grave danger in referral is that the church leader will feel that having sent his counselee off to the welfare agency, to join Alcoholics Anonymous, or to be interviewed by the psychiatrist, his responsibility is ended. This is not so. The people to whom the referral has been made may desire the church leader's co-operation, and this should be gladly given.

Making a referral is a fine art. It may be of some consolation to the church leader to know that even among the professionals there is a very high casualty rate as they endeavor to refer people for other help. One of the most significant experiences involved in referral is that it will help give the church leader a sense of belonging to a therapeutic team and a feeling that he is co-operating with others in an effort to help his fellow man.

10. Establishing the Counseling Relationship

AFTER THE exploratory encounter the counselor will feel that he can or cannot help this person. If he feels that he can help him, then it is important that he talk with the prospective counselee concerning the action involved in the counseling process. This is called "structuring the relationship."

The Expectations of the Counselee

There should be an initial understanding of some of the peculiarities of a counseling relationship. It is quite different from any other kind of relationship between two people. As a counselee comes for counseling, he has certain anticipations. These expectations will be different from those of normal social relationships and will bear closer examination.

The expectation of dependency.—When a person comes to a counselor for help, it is an admission that he has a problem which he cannot solve without the aid of another. This contrasts with the pattern of our culture where man is expected to be self-sufficient and capable of handling every unforeseen condition.

This expectation may be a strong motivating force toward counseling, but the ultimate objective of the counselor is the independence of his counselee. Therefore, the expectation of dependency should be temporary and gradually cease to exist as the relationship proceeds.

The expectation of self-orientation.—In a counseling relationship the counselee expects the discussion to center upon him—his life, his problems, and his difficulties are to be the focus of attention. This, too, is different from a normal social relationship, since someone who continually talks about himself is considered an ill-mannered bore.

The expectation of nonretaliation.—In a good counseling situation the counselee should feel that the counselor will not strike back at him. The counselee should feel that he can speak with complete confidence. Moreover, he should feel that he can speak of subjects not generally discussed in polite company. The church leader says in effect, "You can talk about anything you want to, no matter how bad or vulgar it seems." Johnson calls this "unconditional love," and though it is essential to counseling in general, it has a particular application to counseling in a church setting.

Establishing Boundaries

There is always a possibility that the counselee may come to the counseling situation with undue expectations, and it is important to clarify the counseling relationship at the beginning. In Australia, where the great sheep ranches are called stations, men known as boundary riders patrol the property lines of the ranches to keep the sheep on the proper station. Similarly, the pastoral counselor will have to metaphorically ride the boundary. There are boundaries surrounding areas of counseling which need to be carefully defined. Some of the writers refer to this as setting up the limits.

The Boundary of Responsibility

One of the dangers which the church leader faces in counseling is that the expectation of dependency can become a barrier to the counseling process. The counselee thinks of this counselor as an authority figure in church life. Hearing him speak, seeing him before groups, or responding to his leadership may cause the counselee to feel that the church leader is the personification of all knowledge. Such an attitude is very flattering, but it is well to remember the exhortation, "Admit that you do not know everything, for people will soon find it out anyway."

The wise leader will make it clear that he makes no claim to omniscience and that he has no right to make other people's decisions. When Lady Macbeth loses her mind, Macbeth questions the physician with the following:

> Canst thou not minister to a mind diseased,
> Pluck from the memory a rooted sorrow,
> Raze out the written troubles of the brain
> And with some sweet oblivious antidote
> Cleanse the stuff'd bosom of that perilous stuff
> Which weighs upon the heart?[1]

The physician sets up the boundary of responsibility as he says that "therein the patient must minister to himself."

The wisdom of setting up this boundary will be seen when the counselee, having presented his problem, asks the church leader what he should do. The leader can then say: "You remember when we began this counseling process, I told you I did not make other people's decisions. Together we may be able to find the answer."

The Boundary of Time

The leader of a church group must learn that time is a valuable instrument in counseling. Growth takes time. One reason for spacing interviews is that it will allow time for growth. Carl Rogers claims that many of the greatest gains come to a counselee outside the counseling hour. Working with some counselees, it has been discovered that the twelve to fourteen hours following the counseling session are often vital. The counselee continues to grapple mentally with problems discussed with the counselor.

A specific arrangement should be made concerning the boundaries of time. Erickson says, "The establishment of a time arrangement tends to encourage both participants to use the time more wisely."[2] The counselor should tell the counselee that he will be happy to talk with him at specific intervals and for specific periods of time. This time arrangement depends upon the situation and the counselor sets it to suit the particular case. When the allotted time runs out, the counselor can say, "Well, it looks as if our thirty minutes are gone; let's save the rest until our next meeting." This does not mean that the counselor should be inflexible in concluding. However, a good time arrangement will help to save the church leader from long, drawn-out sessions which are generally of little value. It is better to have three thirty-minute periods than one ninety-minute period.

The frequency with which the religious leader sees his counselee requires considerable thought. Among the psychoanalysts, a daily interview is considered necessary. Some psychotherapists see their clients once or twice weekly. The church leader, conscious of his limitations, should not see his counselee too frequently. His counselee needs time to gain insight. In most cases a weekly meeting is probably enough. One pastoral counselor suggests bi-weekly counseling sessions. Generally, the meetings can be more widely spaced as the relationship progresses. In religious counseling, sessions can be fairly short, and a fifteen-minute period may be quite valuable. In consideration of the length of the counseling period, as in other aspects of counseling, each counselee is an individual and must be treated accordingly.

The inexperienced church leader should not be too ambitious. It is better for him to say to the counselee, "I will be happy to chat with you. I suggest we meet four Thursday afternoons for thirty minutes, and at the end of this time we will re-evaluate the situation." The leader needs to be on the alert for the chronic neurotic looking for a crutch upon which to lean. Such a person can take his time and waste his energies. If he specifies the number of interviews, he can evaluate the situation as it develops. At the end of four weeks, he can conclude, refer, or continue. His time boundary saves him from an interminable relationship.

The Boundary of Affection

The boundary of affection is of particular importance in a church setting. When two people come together to talk about highly personal matters, an emotional bond comes to exist between them. Among the psychoanalysts, the bond is referred to as "transference," and it means a feeling of strong attachment if there is a positive transference or a feeling of antagonism if a negative transference.

If a counseling relationship has continued for a period of time and has been productive and worthwhile, a bond will be created. Moreover, this bond will deepen with the passing of time, which makes emotional involvement even more probable. Therefore, a counseling session involving a member of the opposite sex should be handled very carefully. There has been an alarming number of cases in which church leaders with the highest moral principles gradually found themselves drawn into a situation in which they compromised themselves and ruined their ministry.

The dynamics of the emotions engendered toward counseling are very complex; but, at the risk of oversimplification, it can be stated that they are in terms of the counselee's experience. If the experience has been helpful, the counselee may tend to overestimate the counselor. On the other hand, if counseling has caused a confrontation with painful and distressing ideas, a feeling of resentment may develop toward the counselor.

When verbalizations of affection come, the perceptive counselor is careful to indicate that these feelings are *really* toward the counseling situation. At the same time he leaves the way open for the counselee to have a change of mind without feelings of guilt or disloyalty. The following is a situation of this type.

Fredona: You know, Mr. Voyles, this counseling experience has been a great help to me. When I first came here, I felt so depressed and dispirited; but since I have been talking with you, I have found it to be *so* helpful.

Mr. Voyles: Thank you, Fredona. I am glad to know this experience has been helpful. You know that I am anxious to help you in any way I can.

Fredona: This office has become a haven of refuge. Sometimes when things are not going well at work, I think, "Well, never mind, next Tuesday evening I will see Mr. Voyles and I know he will be able to help me." I just wish I could really tell you how I feel about all this. I sometimes wonder . . . if I do not feel too warmly toward you.

Mr. Voyles: Well, Fredona, I hope you realize that you do not feel this way toward me personally. It seems as if you have been helped by our counseling session and that at the moment you feel warmly toward the counseling situation. Now, remember, this feeling is not toward me personally but toward this situation in which you have come to know something of yourself. People sometimes go through experiences like this when they are being counseled. It may be that you will change your mind later on and feel resentful. However, if you do, don't let that worry you. I understand something of the experience through which you're passing.

This interchange helps to clarify the issues, yet leaves the way open for a change of attitude. It also serves as a warning. Mr. Voyles has told Fredona he thinks of this as a counseling relationship and he is not going to become personally involved.

Some professional counselors refuse to see their counselees in any social setting. They do not accept invitations to visit their homes or go to the same social events. The church leader can take this same precaution, but it will be more difficult because of his relationship to the group. If he is too close to the counselee, he will not be as effective in his counseling. He must constantly re-evaluate his relationship to his counselee. Rollo May warns that church leaders are particularly prone to get into trouble in this area and says, "Whenever the counselor finds himself taking subjective pleasure in the presence of the counselee's person, he had better be wary." [3]

Structuring and Restructuring

The concluding portion of the exploratory interview is probably the best time for the counselor to structure the counseling situation. The following is an example of a summarizing statement:

Mr. Burnet: But do you think you can possibly help me?
Counselor: I'll be happy to do what I can, but I am afraid that you might misunderstand what will happen in a counseling relationship. I have a different idea to that of some other people. I hate to admit this, but I do not know everything. Moreover, I do not feel that I can run other people's lives or make decisions for

them. What I am willing to do is to provide an atmosphere in which you can discover yourself, and by a growth experience learn to make the all-important decisions that need to be made. Suppose we arrange to have four conferences on Thursday afternoons from 3:00 to 3:30 P.M. Is that all right with you?

There are a number of implications in the counselor's statement to Mr. Burnet: he tells him of his willingness to be of help in any way that he can; he definitely indicates he does not think he has all the answers; he gives notice that he will not make Mr. Burnet's decisions; he affirms his belief in the growth potential within Mr. Burnet; and he states a definite time so that they will be clear in Mr. Burnet's mind.

In the counseling process these boundaries are sometimes forgotten and it becomes necessary to restate them. This is called restructuring. It may be necessary to tactfully repeat this structuring on a number of occasions.

In this discussion of structuring the situation, the formal establishing of the relationship has been the focus of attention. Structuring provides a framework within which counseling takes place. However, the counseling interview itself is not structured. Here the important word is permissiveness. An effort is made to follow the counselee's leads. The constant endeavor is to help the person discover himself. Nevertheless, it is an advantage to have a well-structured situation in which this permissive relationship takes place.

11. The Heart of the Counseling Process

THE OLDER and more traditional way of counseling was to focus attention on the problem faced by the counselee. After asking a number of very specific questions, the counselor reached conclusions as to the causes of the client's problems. Taking into consideration the causes of his difficulty, his psychological assets and liabilities, and his life situation, the counselor helped his counselee to see the root of his trouble and to formulate a plan of action. Implicit in these procedures was the assumption that the client needed a more rational approach to life.

While it is true that man is a rational creature, his behavior is sometimes very irrational. Man is not so much logical as he is psychological. Attitudes are built up in a multiplicity of ways and because of the emotion involved, it is very difficult to trace their origin. It is fairly easy to give people good reason why they should act in a certain way, but emotional blockages frequently prevent the utilization of this knowledge. An associated difficulty is that the counseling process may have the wrong point of focus. In a previous chapter it was noted that the first problem presented by the counselee is often not the real problem. In fact, the counselee may not even know what his problem is. In *Marriage Consulting*, the authors show that a woman may say, " 'I hate my husband,' and, by the very intensity of her statement, indicate that she loves him very much." [1] Taking the woman's statement literally could easily lead to some most unfortunate circumstances.

Advice-giving in Counseling

Although counselees sometimes make the request, "Please tell me what to do," they really do not seek an impartial answer. They generally want the counselor to confirm their own line of action. If he fails to do so, he becomes the target of their hostility. Counselees are sometimes like the boy explaining to a friend that he was in a dilemma because he did not know which girl to date. The friend suggested flipping a coin, to which the boy replied, "I have done that, but it keeps flipping the wrong one." If the situation has been structured as was suggested in the previous chapter, it will be fairly easy to decline the request to make the other person's decision and refer back to the original contact by saying: "You remember that when we agreed to start this counseling process, I said I did not know all of the answers. I am sorry, but I cannot make decisions for you."

Because the church leader is involved in organizational procedures, it is easy for him to say, "If I were you. . . ." This presents an impossible conjecture. The counselor cannot be this person and because of this impossibility, he should never make decisions which are rightfully the counselee's. A grave, practical issue is that the counselee may hold the counselor responsible for the results of his advice. Rollo May says that advice-giving is not an adequate counseling function because it violates the autonomy of personality.[2] Similarly, Harry Stack Sullivan warns against an easy reassurance:

You cannot do magic with reassuring language. The magic occurs in the interpersonal relations, and the real magic is done by the patient, not by the therapist. The therapist's skill and art lie in keeping things simple enough so that something can happen; in other words, he clears the field for favorable change, and then tries to avoid getting in the way of its development.[3]

All of this involves a basic concept of personality. Gordon Allport states it very clearly in his formulations of the place of the ego in personality. He comments: "Rogers, in effect, asks counselors to sit back with little more than an occasional, well-placed 'M-hm' to encourage the patient himself to restructure and replan his life. The patient's ego takes command. It's about time it should." [4]

Clinebell urges the pastor who ministers to the alcoholic to "stay close to the alcoholic's ego." Considering the question as to how this is to be done, Clinebell says, "Listening, really listening, is basic." [5] Carroll Wise [6] makes a similar emphasis in insisting on neutrality in counseling. If the counselor encourages the counselee to give free vent to his id, or unacceptable impulses, he conveys the idea that the counselee can never be strong and self-sufficient but will always be a victim of his instinctive drives. On the other hand, if the counselor sides with the counselee's conscious or superego, he may help to build up guilt feelings that overpower him and cause him to cower away from the possibility of ever being able to face life alone. Wise suggests a third alternative—an alliance of the counselor with the counselee's ego. He listens with understanding and acceptance to the statements of desires and of guilt. Such listening gives the counselee confidence that he can develop his own resources from within and by growth processes become capable of handling all of life's situations.

Self-Communication

If a counselee does not need someone to give him advice, he certainly needs to say something to himself. When a person is tied in knots, he not only isolates himself from his fellow man but is also divided within himself. Man has a need to communicate with himself. Reinhold Niebuhr calls this the "internal dialogue of self" and says, "We may safely say that the human animal is the only creature which talks to itself." [7] An authority recently suggested that when a person stands up to deliver a lecture he has a twofold purpose. The first and obvious is to convey a message, but he also has a hidden motivation; he wants to hear the sound of his own words, for it is only as he hears himself that he understands what he is really saying. The authority concluded by saying, "How do I know what I think until I hear what I say." [8]

It might be imagined that the ideal way for a person to communicate with himself would be to get into a lonely place and think through his thoughts. This is not necessarily so, for very often during a process like this people grow more lonely, more frustrated, and more at odds within themselves. In the story of Robinson Crusoe there were times when the lonely exile found isolation almost unbearable. When these moments came, he would rush off to a valley on the island and shout into it. Standing there, he could hear the comforting sound of his own voice echoing back to him. People need an echo chamber which enables them to communicate with themselves, and the adept counselor is often the means of providing such an experience.

Dr. Dominick Barbara, the analyst, says, "A good listener will serve as a mirror on which to cast the image of our real selves." [9] The listener gives a person an opportunity to hear himself and to achieve a form of self-communication. In counseling, whenever the counselee speaks, although he may address the counselor, he also tells himself something.

Releasing Expression

Although known intuitively for many years, the value of helping people express themselves has had to be periodically relearned. In the practical outworkings of Freud's techniques, much of his success came from utilizing what Breuer called "the talking cure." Freud had studied with Breuer. A young woman Breuer was treating with hypnosis is quoted as saying, "Dr. Breuer, if you would only let me talk to you and tell you how my symptoms started, I think it would help." Breuer agreed and as she talked on and on, she felt relieved.[10] The patient liked the treatment and called it "the talking cure."

Freud became dissatisfied with hypnotism as a method of psychotherapy and, along with Charcot, developed the cathartic method. This process represented the unburdening of the mind by allowing the emotion of a previously forgotten experience to be expressed. Later, Freud used the technique of free association, as the client in a relaxed position on a couch gave expression to whatever thoughts came into his mind. Through this the client experienced the emotion of forgotten events and allowed the origin of his troubles to be traced.

Necessity for expressing emotions is seen in the physical disorders known as functional. These functional disorders are very painful to the sufferer, although they have no real physical basis. Sometimes this phenomenon is called conversion hysteria. The emotional conflict is converted to a physical, bodily symptom. These are bodily expressions of psychological conflict. Barbara says, "They are forced to find their expressions through a kind of 'organ' language." [11] The emotion needs to be expressed and if there is no other way it may be expressed through the body.

Recognition of the value of expression has come from different forms of psychotherapy. The psychoanalyst works toward an abreaction which will allow his patient to relive a traumatic emotional experience. A counselor with a grief-stricken person helps his subject to go through his grief work, in which he expresses his sense of loss and faces its reality. In marriage counseling ventilation of hostility by the partners is viewed as a necessary step toward adjustment. Working with the alcoholic, an attitude is maintained which permits him to talk it out. Practitioners of client-centered therapy aim at release of expression in the counseling relationship. Some of the best known techniques in therapy, such as play therapy, the use of puppetry, art therapy, and psychodrama, are all founded upon the concept of catharsis.

The Primary Technique

Coming to the heart of the counseling process, it is somewhat humiliating to discover that it is a relatively simple technique. That is, it *seems simple*. In actuality it may be very complicated and involved. The most important technique in counseling is that which allows the counselee to express himself, and, consequently, listening is the heart of the counseling process. Answering the hypothetical question as to how insight development is assisted, Carl Rogers discusses what he calls the *primary* technique: "The answer is bound to be a disappointing one to the overeager. . . . The primary technique is to encourage the expression of attitudes and feelings . . . until insightful understanding appears spontaneously." [12]

Other authorities in the field of human relationships agree on the importance of listening. Belgum says of the nurse and the social worker, "One of the personal and professional qualifications of a nurse is to be able to be a good listener. The social worker is also supposed to be a good professional listener." [13] Similarly, Barbara says, "The psychotherapist's most important tool is listening." [14] In her *Principles of Intensive Psychotherapy*, the great authority Dr. Frieda Fromm-Reichmann says: "What, then, are the basic requirements as to the personality and professional abilities of the psychiatrist? If I were asked to answer this question in one sentence, I would reply, 'The psychotherapist must be able to listen.' " [15]

Having stated the importance of listening, we are immediately faced with the temptation to oversimplify the issues involved. Listening in counseling involves a special sensitivity. Reik, in his book *Listening with the Third Ear*, shows that as the counselor listens to people, he must develop a special responsiveness to the emotional content of their statements. Sensitivity to the emotional overtones will often be the measure of the counselor's skill.

Responses to Feeling

A man talked into the microphone of a tape recorder for the first time. When he heard it played back, a look of incredulity spread over his face. He could not believe that it was his own voice and felt that there must be something wrong with the machine. However, his friends assured him that it was an excellent reproduction. This is a fairly common experience.

Few people realize how their verbalizations sound. Hearing their statements reproduced, they often begin to re-evaluate them. Remembering what has just been said about emotion, it will be seen that one of the main tasks of the effective counselor is that of reflecting emotion. A good counselor is like a mirror or a sounding board, which enables the speaker to see, hear, and ultimately understand himself in a more meaningful way.

Porter suggests that when the counselor makes a response it should be a sort of question which asks of the client, "Do I understand you correctly? Is this what you mean?" [16] If it reflects the client's feelings, it should evoke the immediate reply, "That's right!" The technique is not easy and requires much study if it is to be developed effectively.

Following is the response of a superintendent to a teacher.

Harry: I told you that the doctor advised me to give up my church work, but he really didn't say that. It just seemed at the time that this would be the easy way out.

Superintendent: What you are saying sounds as if you feel pretty bad about this.

The superintendent could have become involved in a discussion of the doctor's diagnosis. However, it is obvious that the Sunday school teacher is concerned about the situation; the wise counselor tries to catch the feelings of guilt and reflect them back.

Another situation is shown in the following:

Mr. Harris: I really enjoy working with those boys. I can hardly wait for the weekly meeting night to come around, but I wonder if a man who is a chain smoker should be working with them. Then, too, there is all this stuff about lung cancer. I know I would be better physically if I gave it up, but I don't think I can. I've tried to so often.

Educational Director: You want to give this thing up, but you don't want to.

Once again it would have been easy for the educational director to become involved in a discussion about smoking. He might have discussed the latest reports about lung cancer. However, the educational director has sensed this man is struggling with ambivalent feelings. Ambivalent simply means feeling two ways about the same thing. Ambivalences can be very painful; and when the church leader clarifies these feelings by a reflective statement, the counselee may come to recognize and accept them.

One counselee describes his reactions to reflective statements: "It is like looking into a mirror for the first time. I never really saw, heard, or felt myself before. It hurt, but it was also a great relief."

Counselor responses should always aim at keeping the counselee talking. One of the well-known techniques is to repeat his last phrase or remark.

Mrs. Carroll: I don't know what is the matter with this church. It used to be different.
Teacher: It used to be different?

The inflection of the voice is of great importance. It says in effect, "Tell me just how you feel about it. I am interested in listening to what you have to say." This inflection is one of the real indications of empathy, as the counselor feels into his counselee's situation.

It is sometimes necessary to ask questions during the counseling procedure. However, the counselor should not convey the impression that he is a lawyer conducting a cross-examination to prove the guilt or innocence of the party. Any idea that he is prying into the counselee's life by questioning may injure the relationship. The form of the question is important, as a question which can be answered with yes or no may block the flow of conversation. A counselor should not ask, "Do you like living with your brother?" One astute writer has suggested that the counselor not ask any save the "tiny little questions."

Learning the art of responsive counseling is not easy. If possible, the trainee counselor should observe a more mature practitioner at work. He will find it profitable to listen to recordings of counseling sessions so that he can catch the inflection of the counselor's voice. It will also help if he reads Carl Rogers' *Counseling and Psychotherapy* and Porter's *An Introduction to Therapeutic Counseling.* Snyder's *A Casebook of Non-Directive Counseling* is particularly good and has an exercise for testing the ability of the reader to make reflective statements.

The realization that man is basically an emotional creature shows the futility of advice-giving. The counselee needs to develop ego-strength and self-communication. The primary technique for facilitating expression is that of listening, and for this the counselor must develop a mental set peculiar to the counseling situation. Emotional overtones are of vital importance, and the counselor does his best work as he reflects emotion to the counselee, which enables him to take appropriate action.

12. A Successful Conclusion

COUNSELING is never an end in itself, despite the satisfactions which it may bring to both the counselor and the counselee. A recent article in a national magazine told of a fifteen-year relationship of a psychoanalyst and his client, during which time the client showed no improvement. Unfortunately, some have taken this as an indictment of all counseling procedures. Psychoanalysis is a highly specialized form of psychotherapy and should never be confused with simple counseling. For the church leader, counseling is a simple, brief procedure which is to help people and should never become an end in itself.

Some years ago a wise professor, speaking of parent-child relationships, said that the main task of parents is to prepare their children to get along without them. So it is with counseling. The counselor always has independence as the goal of his counselee. This independence is generally closely associated with the idea of insight.

Levels of Insight

There is much confusion in defining insight. English and English describe it as "reasonable understanding and evaluation of one's own mental processes, reactions, abilities; self-knowledge." [1] This definition will serve as a starting point, but there are some important considerations that serve to refine the concept.

Insight should not be confused with explanation. The counselee may offer many explanations for his behavior and give reasons for it, but these need not have any dynamic significance. In fact, rationalization is a well-known psychological mechanism used by people who offer plausible explanations for their behavior and are unwilling to understand the feelings and conflicts giving rise to their difficulties. Finding good reasons for behavior often tends to block real growth in understanding.

Neither does interpretation by the counselor necessarily lead to insight. As the counselor listens to his counselee, the source of trouble may seem obvious and he often feels that he should reveal this to his counselee. Rather unfortunately, this interpretation may only represent the counselor's own comprehension of the problem and have no meaning for the counselee. If the counselee sees the counselor as an authority figure, he may accept his interpretation without thinking any more about the real dynamics. Carroll Wise suggests that the counselor should endeavor to restrain himself in the giving of interpretations. He comments: "If the counseling procedure is successful the person will make his own interpretation spontaneously and in the long run these interpretations will be the most helpful." [2]

Insight must always be thought of in terms of development. Four levels in the development of insight have been suggested:

Awareness of need.—Coming to feel that he has a problem, the individual seeks help.

The individual's perception of external relationships.—He begins to see his problem in terms of his relationship to others, often blaming them for his difficulty.

Internal perception.—The individual begins to focus his attention upon himself and to see his own feelings and motivations.

Exploration.—The individual makes efforts to explore possible solutions for his difficulties. [3]

Process of Insight

Possibly the most fallacious idea about insight is that once the counselee has had this sudden, dramatic experience, everything is clear to him and he has no more problems. The picture in the minds of many people is that of a prisoner in his psychological cell, feeling his way along the wall, and suddenly his touching some hitherto unknown spot causes the wall to fly open, revealing an exit through which he walks into the sunlight as a free man in a new world. So, in the counseling experience it is alleged that there comes the great moment of truth, and from that moment the counselee has no more difficulties in adjusting to life.

If this picture is to be closer to reality, it needs elaboration. The man standing alongside the open door finds the dazzling sunlight almost blinding, and covering his eyes with his hands, he makes a strategic retreat into the gloomy corner of his cell. For a time he may prefer to remain in this safe place and later regain the courage to face the outside world again. However, there are still moments when the burden of light and freedom become too great and he longs for, and even returns to, the security of his cell.

Counseling is an educational process which tends to have an uneven development. In any learning process students may progress rapidly, then remain stationary or even regress before making a new thrust forward. Sometimes after a period of regression, facts become clear, concepts are more easily handled, and fresh progress takes place. The counselor must not be discouraged by temporary reverses. If he realizes these are part of the total process, he will not let them become a source of anxiety.

Factors in Insight

One of the best summaries of insight is given by Carl Rogers in his book *Counseling and Psychotherapy*. He states that insight consists of the perception of relationships, the acceptance of self, and the element of choice. A brief examination of these will follow.

The perception of relationships.—The troubled person is in a state of disorganization. For him life is like a jumbled, jigsaw puzzle. Although the facts are known to him, emotional blockages have kept him from seeing the relationship between these facts. With the developing counseling relationship and the resulting reduction of emotional barriers, life's jigsaw pieces begin to fit into an interlocking pattern. Cause and effect tie-ins become more obvious and make sense. Alternative lines of possible procedure, formerly unrealized, become more clearly defined.

The acceptance of self.—Every person has three images: the person he thinks he is, the person he would like to be, and the person he actually is. As the counseling relationship develops, it is no longer necessary for the counselee to present the socially acceptable, but unreal, self-image to the counselor. In the development of counseling he is able to drop his defenses and accept himself as he is. Allport refers to this as part of the process of maturing and calls it "self objectification." He quotes Socrates as saying on one occasion, "I must first know myself." [4] Very often, as counseling proceeds, the counselee may admit his own shortcomings and set up more realistic goals. Understanding and acceptance of self is a very important part of a developing insight.

The element of choice.—Whether insight or activity comes first is a moot question. Some people feel that when a counselee follows a new plan of action and experiences its satisfaction, he begins to realize the reasons for his previous unsatisfactory behavior. We are all familiar with people who can theorize about their behavior, yet seem to have little power to do anything about reorganizing their lives. Allport says, "But for any basic change, insight must be supplemented by a new orientation, a vigorous plan for the future, a new and effective motivation." [5] For this reason, real insight is sometimes referred to as the creative will. Faced with two ways of satisfying his needs, the person with insight accepts the adult way, bypassing immediate and temporary satisfaction for delayed but more permanent satisfaction.

Techniques in Assisting Insight

Rather unfortunately, there are no simple techniques for helping one to develop insight. The whole counseling process is involved, but there are a few ideas which could be of value:

(1) Encourage the expression of attitudes and feelings. "It [insight] comes in part as an individual is allowed to be spontaneous and finds that his own spontaneous feelings or ideas have a value to himself and to another person." [6]

(2) Sometimes a summary of what has been said or has taken place in the counseling conference can help.

(3) The focusing of attention upon some aspect of the problem can be tactfully done, enabling the counselee to explore that particular area more thoroughly.

(4) The clarification of alternatives and what might be their possible outcomes may help with developing insight.

(5) Even though basically opposed to interpretation, Carl Rogers agrees that there may be some part that interpretation can play in helping with the developing insight.

The Problem of Concluding

One of Stephen Leacock's most amusing short stories is about the curate who could not say good-by. It recounts the experience of a curate who had great difficulty in terminating a conversation. Before departing on a two-week vacation, as part of his pastoral duties, he made a visit to a certain home. When he felt he had remained long enough, he arose to go. His hostess politely urged him to stay, and he agreed. This went on all day until he finally decided to remain for supper. The husband came home from work; the process started again and continued right through the evening. Ultimately, the curate remained for the whole of his vacation and only death brought a final release. While there might be few cases that would be as extreme as this, the successful conclusion of a counseling relationship often concerns the beginning counselor.

The unsuccessful case will probably cause some anxiety to the beginning counselor. He cannot succeed with everybody. It will be much better for him if he recognizes this and does not feel a neurotic compulsion always to be successful. If, after several interviews, he sees that the relationship is not going well, it is probably best to terminate it. The following is an illustration of such an experience.

Mrs. Webb: This is not an easy thing to say, but I'm afraid I'm not getting anything out of these interviews. I know you are really trying to help me, but. . . .

Counselor: I wonder about that myself. It doesn't seem as if our relationship is going too well. It may be my fault. Why don't we just terminate it for the present. Perhaps we can get together later if that would be helpful.

The counselee's guilt is allayed, and the counselor outwardly acknowledges that he is willing to share the blame for what may have gone wrong. However, once again he leaves the door open in case help can be given later.

It has already been noted that it is good technique in setting up a counseling relationship to stipulate a number of meetings which can vary anywhere between two and six. If this structuring is properly done, it is relatively easy to bring the relationship to a successful conclusion.

Mr. Mazy: I am very grateful to you for having taken this time with me.

Superintendent: I am glad to have been of help. You will remember that in the beginning we agreed on four conferences and this is the fourth. This might be a good place for us to finish. You will always remember that I am willing to be of help at any time that I can.

This helps in a number of ways. The counselor is able to avoid giving his counselee a feeling of rejection. It also helps the counselee who sometimes feels guilty about indicating that he no longer needs the counselor.

The counselor should remember that his goal is for his counselee to become autonomous. Sometimes counselors have a strange feeling of disappointment in discovering that the counselee is able to get along without them. The sweetest words to a counselor's ears should be, "I think I can manage on my own. I am grateful for the help that you have given me."

Part Three

Specialized
Considerations

THE PRINCIPLES of counseling as set out in the second section of this book are applicable to many areas. The trainee-counselor who has mastered the general over-all techniques has tools that he can use in almost any given situation. However, after a consideration of the over-all technique, it is profitable to go into the distinctives of some specialized areas.

Counseling the sick is an important ministry for the layman. Chapter 13 shows the psychological reactions of sick people, then indicates the special resources which the layman has in ministering to a sick person. The idea of a therapeutic team is advanced so that the layman can learn to respect the work of others who are ministering to the sick. Vital ministries to the convalescent and bereaved are discussed as challenging opportunities for service for the layman.

The terrifying deterioration of family life is a challenge to all Christians. Is this area too specialized for the layman? Experiences in England have led observers to answer no. For the layman who would endeavor to help in this vital area, there are important principles which are reviewed in chapter 14.

There are generally more women than men working as volunteers within churches, and they are increasingly assuming positions of leadership. Are these women good counselors? There are both assets and liabilities in femininity as far as counseling is concerned, and several aspects of this question are explored in chapter 15.

This book is only the beginning. It is the sincere desire of the writer that it will serve as an inspiration to laymen to learn more. To help in this procedure, attention is paid to the directive, non-directive, and eclectic theories of counseling; books helpful in learning counseling are referred to; and the possibility of learning from personal theory all form part of the concluding chapter of the book.

13. Counseling the Sick

PROBABLY ONE of the most important areas in which the church leader can counsel will be with people who are ill. Most ministers find it almost impossible to make the number of visits to the sick which should be made. Consequently, this is an important field of service for the layman.

Russell L. Dicks has written a book to help laymen undertaking this work. In his Foreword, he emphasizes the responsibility of this task because of the harm that the layman can do in visiting the sick. He says, "This booklet is written in defense of the sick, in an effort to protect them from the well-meaning, but misdirected efforts of visitors." [1] Most people who have worked in hospitals have known well-meaning religious workers who see the immobilized patient as either an opportunity for fervent evangelism or a captive audience for recounting personal experiences in the field of medicine, hospitals, or doctors. Fortunately, Dicks goes on to emphasize that there is a great need for visiting the sick. A person's friends may save his life. [2]

This chapter is written in the hope that the harm of which Dicks warns may be avoided, and an essential ministry effectively rendered. Consideration will be given to the psychological reactions that take place within the patient and the resources and techniques of the church worker as he ministers to the sick.

The Crisis of Illness

Illness is not just physical. There are a number of important psychological reactions which should be understood by the person visiting the sick. The church leader who visits an ill person is not expected to know all about the physical aspects of the illness. In fact, it may be better if he knows very little of this. However, it will be of prime importance that he know something about the psychological aspects of the illness, for illness is a time of crises.

Illness is a *social crisis*. The person who is ill is separated from his vocational setting. He is not able to carry on his normal work and, therefore, is absent from the place where he normally spends a good portion of his waking hours. Moreover, he may have financial worries, even though he has some hospitalization insurance. He may also have a considerable amount of anxiety as he ponders being replaced by an ambitious person who is substituting for him.

If the man goes to the hospital, he is removed from his family setting. This may lead to homesickness, for he misses the security of his home—his wife and children, the routine, the home-cooked food. It may seem as if he is living in another world, a world of white-gowned nurses, orderlies, dietitians, and technicians. This may fill him with apprehensions.

Illness is also a *personal crisis*. In sickness there is a tendency for individuals to regress to earlier and more infantile modes of behavior. The patient in the hospital finds himself almost entirely at the mercy of other people. In this dependent situation, it is easy for him to fall back into ways and attitudes of his childhood. His body becomes the focus of attention of the doctors, technicians, and nurses who are constantly taking his temperature, counting his pulse rate, inquiring about his movements, and so on. It is little wonder that the patient sometimes becomes obsessed with his bodily functions, and that his reactions to them are almost infantile.

The experience of pain can be threatening. Too little attention has been given to this factor. As Wayne Oates puts it, "This is followed by shock, pain hits the patient. It carries with it a stunning, shocking effect." [3] This experience with pain, particularly if it is over a long period of time, can have a debilitating effect upon the personality of the sick person. The threat to life and the experience of pain may unite to cause what Oates calls "the return

of the repressed." [4] In this experience, repressed emotional conflicts often flood into consciousness, giving rise to feelings of guilt.

After the experience of illness comes convalescence, which has
a relationship to the regression which took place during the
critical period of illness. As health is restored and the patient is
able to accept responsibility, he discovers that he has to relinquish
some of his dependent and egocentric infantile reactions.

Convalescence has been likened to growing up, for there are
many resemblances between it and adolescence. Sometimes, like
the adolescent, the convalescent tries to develop too quickly,
wrenching himself free from dependency and accepting respon-
sibilties for which he is not yet fitted. On other occasions, he can
be like the adolescent, yearning for adult life, yet unsure of himself. He wistfully longs for health but is so demoralized that he is
unwilling to accept it.

When the church worker seeks to help in this crisis, he should
realize that the sick person may manifest personality characteris-
tics that are quite different from those which characterized him
before his illness.

The Resources of the Church Leader

There are a number of resources which are unique to the
church leader in his ministry to the sick. Although not as sym-
bolically significant as the minister, he has values within his own
person.

The church leader represents someone who cares. The patient
is very often isolated on an island of pain and is out of touch with
other people. Frequently, doctors, nurses, and orderlies are hurrying about with their duties; but the religious worker comes and
says, "I have no professional stake in your case. I am interested in
you personally." This may give him an advantage over the busy
minister who rushes in and out of the sick room. While the minister will probably be tremendously important to the patient, there
may also be the lurking suspicion that he is visiting because it is a
part of his job. With the layman, there is no suspicion. He is there
because he cares.

The church leader represents someone who heals. Improvement may come to the patient because of his call. Recent developments in the concept of psychosomatic medicine have helped us to see the close interaction of body and mind.

A serene spirit can be of inestimable value in the healing of the body. Once again the simple technique of listening is important. Russell Dicks says, "There is an art to visiting in the sick room. Being able to listen is more than half the art." [5]

The patient has been quiescent for so long that he is often just longing to talk with someone. Instructions have been given to him, he has been told what, when, and how to eat, and often feels as if he is surrounded by a veil of secrecy. Now the church worker says in effect, "Tell me how you feel." In listening he helps the patient to express his hostilities and fears, thus clearing the emotional blockages and possibly facilitating the healing process. (A review of chapters 5 and 6 of this book will be helpful at this point.)

The church worker also represents someone who needs the patient. As a representative of the church, he invites the sick person to become a part of a religious community in which people are concerned for each other. If the patient already belongs to the religious community, the worker comes to emphasize that others in the group are concerned about him. Within this fellowship there is a tremendous growth potential.

Another resource which is peculiar to the religious worker is the Bible. The Bible is the most ancient of all literature and contains the record of the struggles of men and women with the vicissitudes of life. In its pages are to be found the experiences of men and women of faith in their encounter with suffering, affliction, and adversity. Consequently, there is much to encourage and help the modern sufferer.

Passages such as the twenty-third Psalm, the fourteenth chapter of John, the eighth chapter of the epistle to the Romans, have enshrined in them great words which have been a source of comfort through the years and often bring reassurance when nothing else can. Some particularly good portions of the Scriptures to use with sick people are: Psalm 90:1-2,4; Psalm 121; Matthew 6:25-27; Matthew 6:28-34; Philippians 4:6-7,13,19. When the Scriptures are read to the sick person, it is important to keep the passage short.

The visitor to the sick should commit to memory some of the great passages of the Scriptures so that he will be able to quote them if a crises arises. As he stands by the bedside, it is of great help for him to be able to repeat such statements as, "The eternal God is thy refuge, and underneath are the everlasting arms" (Deut. 33:27); or "Peace I leave with you, my peace I give unto you: not as the world giveth, give I unto you. Let not your heart be troubled, neither let it be afraid" (John 14:27).

Sometimes it is advisable to leave a verse of Scripture with the patient. Bonnell suggests "spiritual prescriptions"—appropriate verses of Scripture written on a card or a piece of paper. The visitor may say, "When you are ill, the doctor gives you a prescription for some medicine which will help you. Now I want to give you a spiritual prescription which will help you." For months after her illness one woman was observed to be carrying in her purse a battered "spiritual prescription." She later recounted what a benefit it had been for her to have these words upon which to focus her attention during her trying illness.

Prayer, intelligently used, can have therapeutic value in a ministry to the sick. In a survey conducted among hospital patients as to what they expected when a minister visited them, 51 per cent said that above all things they thought the minister should "have prayer." It is not easy for the visitor to know when he should pray. He will have to learn to gauge the situation. The visitor of the sick should "feel the spiritual pulse" of the patient. This can be done by noting if he has a Bible or religious literature or if in his conversation he indicates that he would appreciate such a ministry. In the final analysis, it will have to be a matter of sensitivity to the total situation.

There are a number of factors which make up a satisfactory sick-room prayer. The prayer should be offered in a conversational tone of voice and should not be too long. Young suggests about as many phrases as are contained in the twenty-third Psalm. Familiar verses of Scripture may be used and will help to stimulate the patient's faith. The Christian attitude towards suffering may be clarified in a helpful way, and without creating magical expectations, a healthy optimism can be engendered. There can be no fixed type of prayer as each situation will call for an individual handling. An example of one prayer is:

Oh Lord our God, we come to thee in the name of the Great Physician to pray for thy blessing upon our brother. Grant to him that he will know that thou hast said, "Lo, I am with you alway," and that in this experience, as in all of life, we can know that "all things work together for good to them that love God." Give thy guidance to nurses and doctors, the sense of thy presence to those whom he loves, and healing to his body and spirit. Through Jesus Christ our Lord.

Good literature for the patient will be helpful. It can be left with him and will serve to remind him of the visit and provide something for him to turn to during his lonely hours. Although many materials have been prepared for this purpose, selections should be carefully made. The reading material should be on good paper, contain a message of comfort and encouragement, be attractive in format, and of light weight so that it will not be too difficult to hold. Often literature will serve as a good conversation piece.

Rules for Visiting the Sick

In pastoral counseling there is presently an emphasis on the idea of the healing team. The minister is made to see that he is a part of a team of professional people who are ministering to the patient. Similarly, the layman should see himself as working with this team, even though there is no formal recognition of the fact. Since this activity is generally carried on in an institutional setting, there must be respect for the essential organizational procedures within the institution.

Abbreviated from Richard Young's *The Pastor's Hospital Ministry*, the following procedures may be helpful to the layman who visits the sick.

(1) It is a good policy in general visiting not to go into any room where the door is closed without first finding out something of the circumstances that exist behind that door. . . .

(2) Be very careful to note "No Visiting" and "Isolation" signs hanging on the door. . . .

(3) Look to see if the light is on over the patient's door, and if it is, do not enter at all until the nurse has taken care of the patient's needs. . . .

(4) Do not touch the patient's bed. . . .

(5) Size up the entire situation at a glance during the process of entering the room. . . .

(6) Always let the patient take the lead in shaking hands. . . .

(7) Upon entering the room take a position, whether sitting or standing, in line with the patient's vision so that he is not required to move around in the bed. . . .

(8) Beware of letting the visit become a pathological conference. . . .

(9) Help the patient to relax. . . .

(10) Do not carry emotional "germs" from one room to another. When one has listened to a sordid confession or dealt with any highly charged emotional situation, [get rid of the emotional effects] before going to the next patient. . . .

(11) Do not reveal negative emotional reactions through the voice, countenance, or manner. . . .

(12) [Do not] visit when [you are] sick. . . .

(13) Do not make a visit too long. . .

(14) Don't whisper or speak in low tones to a nurse, to a member of the family or to anyone else in the sickroom or near it, if there is the slightest chance that the patient will see you or hear you. . . .

(15) As a general rule, . . . leave when the patient's meal is delivered to his room. . . .[6]

Counseling the Convalescent and the Chronically Ill

Hospital stays have been considerably shortened over the years. This was brought about in the first place by necessity, but experience has proved that it is not desirable that people should remain in hospitals for long periods if it can be avoided. However, the patient upon returning home sometimes finds himself in an awkward situation. He has been in the hospital for some time, lost much of his strength, and is fearful or apprehensive. Oftentimes the problems of convalescence are more psychological than physiological.

Similar to the convalescent is the person who is chronically ill. The sudden illness, with the drama of surgery and hospitalization, attracts attention; but as the illness stretches into weeks, months, and years, it is easy for people to forget. Though more prolonged, in many ways ministry to these individuals will be similar to that of the convalescent. Consequently, much of what is said will apply to both the convalescent and the chronically ill.

It was previously noted that often the period of convalescence is like growing up all over again. The church leader can be a great help during this period. An awareness of the problems peculiar to the convalescent will aid the layman in a more effective ministry.

The attitude which the convalescent has toward his illness will be of great importance. One convalescent may endeavor to overcome his problems and to accept life's responsibilities, while another may enjoy his dependance upon others.

A great problem with the chronically ill is the feeling of isolation and loneliness. Previously the center of all attention in the hospital, it now seems as if nobody cares. There are long, lonely, and isolated hours. In certain types of chronic illnesses, there are peculiar difficulties. Even with a thoroughgoing philosophy of life, the anticipation of future pain or a crippling disease, as is the case with arthritis and similar conditions, can be threatening.

Life must be reorganized for many of the chronically ill. The amputee, for example, particularly needs support for the difficulties which he faces. The church leader must face this challenge with great courage, as it is in this area that his ministry will probably be most significant. A strong, vibrant faith and a belief that miracles can happen are necessities. The church leader should be sympathetic, supporting, understanding, and yet know the correct time to issue a challenge to a person wallowing in self-pity.

Particular assistance may be rendered in occupational therapy by helping to interest the convalescent in hobbies which will help to fill the lonely hours and foster his creative capacities. Literature can also be provided. The convalescent may have wanted to read for years, but never had a chance. Now he has the chance but may need someone to guide him in making his selections.

Above everything else, during this period of enforced idleness, the convalescent can very often think the long thoughts. A listening ear and an understanding heart may give the church worker his supreme opportunity for a meaningful ministry.

Ministering to the Bereaved

In ministering to the sick, the church leader will find that he has a wider ministry than just to the person who is ill. Sometimes he may find himself ministering to the nurse or the doctor in his sickroom contacts. However, next to the patient himself, the patient's family is the most important group that calls for the leader's attention. This is especially true in bereavement. When the doctor and other members of the healing team have completed their responsibilities, the family is left alone with their sense of loss. It is now that the religious worker comes with his special ministry.

The minister of the church plays a very important role in arranging the burial services. He can be of great help as the family passes through this experience. One of the tragedies of the ministry is that after the funeral the pastor may feel that only one visit to the family is sufficient. However, studies have shown that grief lasts long after separation from a loved one. Dr. Lindemann, the psychiatrist who worked with the relatives of victims of the Coconut Grove fire, concluded that five or six interviews were necessary to help a person through an experience of grief. This should be the minimum number of calls the church worker should plan, if he is to be of real help.

As the church leader seeks to minister to the grief-stricken, there are at least six things which he should keep in mind.

Glib assurance is of little value.—Church workers very often have a tendency to be unduly reassuring, as they try to help grief-stricken people. Some workers can become aggressive in their emphasis on the Christian hope and cause the person to feel guilty because of his pain at parting from a loved one. It is far better to accept the fact of sorrow and agree that the experience is going to be painful and trying.

Do not try to divert the sorrowing.—It hurts to see a person grieve. Our immediate reaction is to try to save some one from pain and ourselves from the difficulty of watching him suffer. A pastor who worked with a group of college students had to break the news to a girl of the accidental death of her father. Speaking later with the students who had helped her prepare for the journey home, he asked what they had done. A spokesman from the group volunteered the information that every time the girl began to cry they immediately introduced another subject so that she would not have time to think about her bereavement. This typical reaction is felt to be a real ministry to the bereaved person. It is what one writer calls "trying to camouflage death." The reality of death must be faced; there is no sense in trying to avoid it.

Grief needs to be expressed.—Many people feel that the deceased person should not be mentioned. However, Jackson says, "The bereaved may want to review the relationships with the deceased. Just talking about these relationships with someone who listens sympathetically is usually adequate." [7]

Dr. Lindemann has developed the concept of "grief work." There is a certain pain which comes with grief and this pain must be faced. A lot of this grief work takes place as the bereaved person expresses himself. Writing about the needs of the bereaved in *Pastoral Psychology*, William F. Rogers sees one of the needs of the bereaved person as the expression of sorrow and sense of loss.[8] As the bereaved person repeats the story of his loss to others, he becomes increasingly aware of the reality of his loss and comes to a healthier acceptance of it.

Guilt feelings should be accepted.—Often there is a sense of guilt and a feeling that responsibilities to the loved one might have been evaded. Sometimes there is a basis for this, but on most occasions this is not true. Whatever the situation, the feelings of the grief-stricken should be accepted.

Help to establish new relationships.—Sooner or later the bereaved person must break loose from the image of the lost one and begin to establish new relationships. The church leader can be of particular help as he endeavors to enlist this person in the organizations of the church. The Christian fellowship offers unique opportunities for new and vital interpersonal relationships.

In concluding this chapter it will be noted that the Christian faith has made the care of the sick its particular responsibility. When the church worker engages in visitation of the sick, he is becoming involved in one of the most meaningful activities of the church and is joining hands with him who is known as the Great Physician.

> The healing of His seamless dress
>   Is by our beds of pain;
> We touch Him in life's throng and press,
>   And we are whole again.

14. Marriage and Family
Counseling

MARRIAGE is more popular today than ever before. In 1890, only 55 per cent of the population of the United States was married. By 1940, 61 per cent was married. Upon reaching the age of forty-five years, nine out of every ten people will have been married.

Unfortunately, in this time when marriage is so popular, it is also tragically true that family life is less stable than ever before. Today's family is in trouble. Howard Whitman has dramatized this by saying, "More than a thousand times every day somewhere in the United States, a judge's gavel falls and with two words, 'Divorce granted,' somebody's love story comes to an end." [1] This is of great concern to the church. It must do something to stop the deterioration of family life and help to build Christian concepts into this basic sociological unit.

The Layman Functioning As a Marriage Counselor

Skidmore, Garret, and Skidmore list friends and relatives, public advisors, the clergyman and other religious leaders, doctors, nurses, lawyers, educators, social workers, and professional marriage counselors as people involved in marriage counseling. Very few of these people have had specialized training for the task; yet, they are by necessity involved in the process.

When people are in trouble, very few of them are able to contact a professional marriage counselor. One study in Kansas of dismissals of divorce complaints indicated that ten out of the

116

fifteen had discussed the matter with relatives and friends before terminating the proceedings. None had consulted a psychiatrist or a marriage counselor. A similar study with students showed that 80 per cent took their troubles to relatives and friends.

Dr. David R. Mace,[2] in telling of the commencement of the marriage counseling movement in England, shows that there has been a wide use of lay people. Forced by financial exigencies, in the first place, to bypass professional help, lay people were carefully selected. The primary criterion of fitness was a test of personality, applied without discrimination as to previous training and qualification. Many of these lay people would probably be rejected on academic grounds in American institutions, but the evaluation of psychiatrists, after examining the work of seven hundred counselors, was that the standard of the lay people was equally as good as that of the professionals.

The reaction of the British public to the lay counselor has been significant. Many of the people claim that the lay counselor is more accessible than the professional, who always appears to be too busy to listen to them. The counselees also seemed encouraged by the fact that the counselor was doing his work voluntarily, because he cared, not because he was being paid. One psychiatrist in working with lay counselors found that often people were more at ease with the layman because they felt that he was on their side. Altogether, Mace's picture of the place of the layman is a very challenging one.

The recently published *Americans View Their Mental Health* tells of a survey of the problems faced by people in America today.[3] The report shows that 42 per cent of those reporting have problems with their marriage and 12 per cent have trouble with their children. In the section on sources of help, the report shows that 42 per cent of those seeking assistance consulted clergymen; 29 per cent, physicians in general; 18 per cent, psychiatrists or psychologists; and 10 per cent, social agencies or marriage clinics. So, while most of the problems had to do with marriage and family, only a few of these went to professional marriage counselors, while most of them turned to the church leader for help.

As hard as the church leader may work in this area, he is inevitably faced with a difficulty. The pastor cannot do it all. He already has far too many responsibilities, and Wynn suggests that if he is to cope with the situation there are two steps that he needs to take:

(1) the organization of his daily work around the integrating principle of ministering to Christian families; and then (2) the training of parents and leaders of the parish to work at their God-given task. For some this is a radical re-orientation; but in that direction lies a rewarding pastorate.[4]

Developing the idea further, Wynn places much of this responsibility, i.e., the task of adult education, on the educational program of the church.

Even if the pastor were willing and able to counsel all who came to him, there would still be a complication. Sometimes people who are having marriage difficulties feel hostility toward their minister. If the minister has not given premarital counseling, there may be resentment. In a moving, anonymous letter to a Christian paper, the writer made a plea for compulsory premarital counseling. As he did this, he revealed his resentment that no effort was made to give him adequate counseling before the marriage relationship took place. The important point is that the man did not seek premarital counseling, but felt antagonistic because it was not given.

Frequently, the minister is not to blame, but this attitude prevents the couple's turning to him, whereas the lay leader can take up the task of helping perhaps a fellow class member to work through his unreasonable attitude. Such help may be rewarded by the couple's reaching a position of objectivity in their attitudes and turning to their pastor for counsel in their deteriorating marital relationship.

Many sociologists have commented upon the deterioration of family life and laid much of the blame at the feet of urbanization. They have argued that in the small rural communities the social pressures help to keep the family together. With the movement of people to the cities, families are much more detached. Some have claimed that for the first time in history responsibility for making a marriage work has been placed upon the shoulders of just two people.

What is the responsibility of the church to these urban communities? The modern Sunday school class, as seen in Southern Baptist churches, lays great emphasis upon the small intimate groups. Within these groups there are pressures which could help to overcome some of the difficulties resulting from urbanization.

Church groups can often exercise a preventative ministry in the area of marital difficulties by making possible the development of mutual friends and activities. In a church in a college town, the superintendent of the Young Married People's department goes to great trouble to have a biweekly social function. There is very little expense, a nursery is provided for the children, and many a struggling young couple feels that the church social life is a vital factor in helping to keep their marriage intact. One Sunday school teacher not only involves the members of her class within the group activities of the class program but also has an excellent, flexible program of social activities for the group. If she hears of trouble, she quickly schedules extra social events and involves the troubled couple in them. This may be only a stopgap, but it often helps the situation until other steps can be taken.

The lay worker in the church will often find his marriage counseling done in an incidental way. A church deacon seeking a subscription to the budget may finish his interview by showing the parishioner his psychological assets and liabilities in his family relations; a Sunday school teacher trying to tell the message of the prodigal son's returning to his Heavenly Father may help a prodigal father to assume a new responsibility for his son; and a church leader's concern for the family of God might easily make a new and significant contribution to the Jones family.

Principles of Marriage Counseling

Coming more specifically to the formalized concepts of marriage and family counseling, it is noted that there are three important areas. First is *premarital*. This includes dating, petting, distinguishing between love and infatuation, sex attitudes, selecting a partner, and any factor which leads to marriage. The second area is *marital*, which has to do with the relationship between husband and wife, and includes sexual adjustment, planned parenthood, finances, in-laws, social life, and similar aspects. The third area is *family* counseling and takes in all that is involved in husband-wife-children relationships.

Each of these areas will offer opportunities for the lay worker within the church.

Without envisaging himself as a professional marriage counselor, it is advisable for the church leader to become familiar with some of the principles involved in marriage counseling. Dr. Fosdick once stated, "Personal counseling, therefore, like marriage, is 'not to be entered into unadvisedly or lightly.' " [5] The principles which follow will help the church worker to understand some of the dynamics involved in marriage and family counseling.

The distinctive feature of marriage counseling is the interaction of two personalities.—In personal counseling the aim is to help the individual know himself and learn to adjust to his environment. Marriage counseling seeks to facilitate the relationship of two people to each other. Each of these people may have fairly good emotional health, but their interpersonal relationship is sick. It is important that a channel of communication be opened between the two partners. Much of the difficulty may come from their inability to discuss their problems.

Some highly trained counselors are not successful in marriage counseling because they place too much emphasis on the mental health of the individual rather than the mutual adjustment of two people. Marriage is a partnership which requires continual compromise, and each partner must shorten his personal objectives and accept limitations in order that a mutually beneficial relationship may be realized.

The marriage counselor must constantly remind himself that he is working with a relationship between two people. Most of the techniques used in marriage and family counseling are similar to those set out previously in this book, with the essential modification of the adjustment of two people to each other.

The ventilation of feelings is vital.—People who have been involved in courtship, marriage, and family problems often become emotionally overwrought. When emotion builds, there must be some means of release; and counseling provides this opportunity. Reference should be made to chapters 4, 5 and 11 where the dynamics and techniques of this process are discussed. The counselor should endeavor to structure the relationship in such a manner that the counselee does not feel guilty about expressing hostility. Sometimes this experience is referred to as the reduction of hostility.

The counselor should maintain a strict neutrality.—When a husband or wife feels antagonistic toward a spouse, he or she will sometimes seek to enlist sympathy from another person. They often come to the counselor expecting him to take sides in the matter. The perceptive counselor will avoid being manipulated or maneuvered into a position where his counselee can call upon him as an ally against the spouse.

The marriage counselor must never allow himself to become judge, jury, defendant, or prosecuting attorney. It may be necessary for the counselor to be very specific and tell his counselee that he is completely neutral. Taking care not to indicate an absence of concern, he may have to go on and say that he is concerned for both of them and wants to act accordingly.

Joint interviews should not be prematurely attempted by the lay counselor.—Because the counselor is attempting to work with a relationship involving two people, he may feel that the best procedure is a joint interview in which both may have an opportunity to express their feelings about the marriage relationship. However, the joint interview is the most difficult of all to undertake. If the inexperienced counselor attempts such a conference, he may find his counselees to be so defensive that the meeting will be futile. On the other hand, they may become brutally frank, and because of the presence of another party, inflict emotional wounds. Mudd warns us that "joint conferences with both partners can be helpful but are difficult and potentially dangerous. They should be undertaken only after careful preparation." [6]

An effective counselor helps to define situations.—Marriage counseling situations are often confusion confounded. In the midst of the chaos of accusations, counteraccusations, and recriminations, it takes a steady mind to help the emotionalized person to have the correct perspective. The counselor, with his permissive attitude, tries to pinpoint difficulties, helps to explore alternatives, and gives oversight to the setting up of goals.

Information can be of value.—The value of information has been previously noted, and also the warning that information should not be given too soon. There are many difficulties which arise in marriage and family relationships through ignorance. When the counselor feels the problem has arisen from a lack of information, he should help the parties concerned to procure the best literature available. This will be particularly true of premarital counseling, when information is needed on such subjects as mixed marriages, sexual problems, birth control, planning to set up a home, budgeting, and similar concerns.

As in other forms of counseling, the counselor leaves the decision in the hands of the counselee.—David Mace expresses this principle in a very fine summarizing statement:

The methods of different counselors vary a good bit, of course, but there are basic principles which most accept. One of these is that the counselor's job is not to tell John and Mary Smith what to do, but to help them find their own solution to their problem. Only a solution that comes from them, out of their own thinking and feeling, is of any use. If the counselor dictated a policy to them, he would be taking over the job of running their lives, impressing his will upon theirs. This he must not do, because the work of the counselor is based upon his respect for the freedom of the individual to manage his own life in his own way, insofar as this is in accord with the welfare of others. [7]

In a church situation the Christian emphasis upon the integrity of the individual demands that we be very careful in the application of this principle.

Marriage counseling has been said to be an expression of our times. In a changing society with the move from a rural to urban way of life, the emphasis on the equality of women, the new freedom given to young people, the anticipation of fulfilment in marriage, and the easy divorce, marriages have had a high casualty rate. The Christian church with its emphasis on the sacredness of the marriage bond and the value of the family unit has found itself faced with new obligations. Ministers can never hope to stem the tide alone; they must call for help. This help can be provided by enlisting a force of lay men and women. Experience in other countries has shown the part that lay people can play. With study, training, supervision and experience, the lay leader can become an important member of the church team which seeks to emphasize the statement of Jesus, "What therefore God has joined together, let no man put asunder" (Matt. 19:6, RSV).

15. The Woman Counselor

AMID THE sociological changes of our day, men and women are trading many of their traditional roles. This sometimes perplexes women as they try to discover their proper role in life. Nowhere is this more clearly seen than in the women who seek to serve within the ranks of the church.

Despite the New Testament declaration that there is neither male nor female in Christ Jesus, in many instances the church has proved to be more prejudiced than any other institution in its attitude toward women. This attitude is illustrated by the celebrated statement of Dr. Johnson: "Sir, a woman preaching is like a dog's walking on his hind legs. It is not done well; but you are surprised to find it done at all." [1]

Precluded from the activities of preaching, many women turn their energies toward missionary activity. It is strange to find in the annals of the modern missionary movement that women who were borbidden to preach at home were permitted to travel to the far-flung corners of the earth to declare the gospel of Christ. This remains true today. One missionary society declares that two-thirds of its missionaries are women. Faced with this perplexity, one denominational leader put it very succinctly, "In the days of the prophet Isaiah, he said 'Here am I, send me.' In our day, a man says, 'Here am I; send my sister.' "

A similar situation existed for many years in the field of social service. A century ago, a young woman of the Church of England wrote to Arthur Stanley, the Dean of Westminster, "I would have given her [the Church] my head, my hand, my heart. She would not have them. She told me to go back and do crochet in my mother's drawing room." [2] Fortunately for posterity, this woman refused to go back and do crochet. She became one of the outstanding women of the ages, for her name was Florence Nightingale. Seemingly she accomplished what she did not only against the blundering officialdom of her day but also against the wishes of her church.

Recognition has come slowly to professional women workers within the churches, but it has recently gathered momentum. The population census for 1950 reported 6,727 women members of the clergy. This represented about 4.1 per cent of the total membership. Statistics of women in law, medicine, and the ministry show that since 1910 there has been a greater increase percentage wise in the ministry. Moreover, there have been many more women employed on church staffs in various capacities which could not be described by the word "clergymen." One authority claims that in religious work some 70 per cent of those involved are women.

In the field of psychotherapy, there have been some outstanding contributions by women. Names like Frieda Fromm-Reichmann, Karen Horney, Anna Freud, and Lauretta Bender come readily to mind. From the point of view of vocational guidance, it has been said, "Although the number of women psychiatrists is still relatively small, this is an excellent field of specialization for women as they are peculiarly fitted for treating the mentally ill." [3]

However, this does not mean that it is easy for a woman to function as a counselor. In an effort to discover something of the dilemma of women counselors, a survey was made of three groups. These included women who were already employed in some kind of professional church work, male and female seminary students who were preparing themselves for professional religious work, and people who were rank and file members of a church. The results of this survey are woven into the discussion which follows.

In the responses of the female professional group to the survey, it became obvious that not many of them were involved in counseling activities which were of any depth. One-third of this group indicated they did not do any counseling. Moreover, those who did counsel apparently carried on their activities at a somewhat superficial level. Fifty-eight per cent of their contacts were one-interview experiences. Two-interview contacts represented 34 per cent of the counseling experiences; three-interview experiences represented 4 per cent of the total; and four-interview contacts represented 4 per cent. None of the respondents indicated seeing people on more than four occasions.

A closer look at the survey indicates that most women who work professionally in churches do not think of themselves as counselors. Asked whether they would prefer to see a man or a woman if they needed counseling, 87 per cent of them indicated that they would prefer a man. Similarly, 64 per cent of them stated that they felt that public opinion was against women counselors.

An examination of the responses of women to this survey helps to deepen the conviction that in church life we are developing an "organizational woman." In some churches it has been the custom in the past to employ women as deaconesses. These women majored in visitation, helped in people's homes, and worked with children and young people. To these women, visitation and personal contacts in the homes were of vital importance. Now it seems that the women workers we are training in our churches are not prepared for this important part of their work. One very capable and outstanding woman worker in a large church writes, "I am not a counselor. My work consists largely in enlisting people and helping to train them." From this and similar expressions, the impression is gained that organization is all-important. This idea may come from the fact that women have a tendency to see themselves as executives within church life.

Counseling is a fairly new field. It is only of comparatively recent years that an attempt has been made to give ministers formal training in counseling. There is still a certain amount of prejudice against a minister's becoming too much involved in such a ministry. It is not unnatural that there should be some prejudices against women entering into this relatively new area.

"If you had a problem would you go to a woman or a man?" The responses of young people answering this question were about evenly divided, indicating that it made little or no difference. Sixty-nine per cent of the adults in a local church expressed their preference for a male counselor. Seventy-eight per cent of the seminary students indicated they would prefer a male counselor. If seminary students have this prejudice, it is easy to understand why people within the church might have difficulty in accepting a woman counselor.

Investigations seem to confirm the fact that women have long been stereotyped as more emotional than men. Johnson and Terman of Stanford University cited fifty of the best studies on sex differences in emotionality, psychoneurotic trends, nervous habits, feelings of inadequacy, etc. They concluded "the results being almost unanimous in indicating less emotional balance in the female." [4] In the groups of professional women church workers surveyed for this article, there was a frank acknowledgement of this difficulty. The disadvantages of women as counselors were stated as follows. They "make everybody's problem theirs;" "become more emotionally involved in problems than a man;" and "find it hard to be impersonal."

In setting out the qualifications for a counselor, Rogers gives a prominent place to objectivity. It easily can be seen that this emotionality may be a definite disadvantage for the woman functioning as a counselor.

However, there is another side to this. Studies carried out in England during World War II showed that very often women were able to stand up to air raids better than men. Moreover, in treatment that followed these nerve-shattering experiences, it was found that women very frequently "bounced back" more quickly than men. This sensitivity of women, coupled with a capacity to regain their psychological equilibrium, could be an asset to them in the all-important factor of empathy in a counseling relationship.

Associated with this is the so-called feminine intuition. Scheinfeld claims that this is part of a woman's training as she matures.

He develops the idea that in all nature the weaker animals have to be more sensitive and alert to dangers if they are to survive. So, woman must learn to observe and interpret little signs or actions which may affect her well-being or relationships with others.

In Annette Garrett's book on interviewing she lists "Things to Look for in Interviewing," such as association of ideas, shifts in conversation, opening and closing sentences, recurrent references, inconsistencies and gaps, and concealed meaning. The mere listing of these indicates an attention to detail which would not be characteristic of most masculine counselors. If these powers of observation and so-called intuition are factually true, this may be an advantage to a counselor, particularly in the area of nonverbal communication.

Another stereotype concerning women counselors is that they talk too much. Zimmerman and Cervantes see women as being compelled to be more loquacious than men. "Women's greater loquacity may likewise be related to the bio-cultural factor that for self-defense she must have more frequent recourse to her tongue than to her fists." [5] In this survey 50 per cent of the female professional church workers stated that women are not good listeners. Generally, there was an indication that they thought women were not good at keeping confidences. If this is true, it certainly will put women at a disadvantage in the counseling field, where the capacity to listen and the ability to keep confidences are vital parts of a successful counseling relationship.

Dingwall has stressed at some length the importance of women in American culture. He states that 75 per cent of our schoolteachers are women and that in the developing of American frontier life, the women occupied increasingly important roles. So he says, "They were still in a sense the guardians of social intercourse, and thus the femininization of American culture was inevitable." [6]

In this survey a number of the professional religious workers stated that a woman had an advantage in counseling because she was seen as a mother figure. It is of interest that these women should have seen themselves in this role. One psychiatrist has said that he could cite the actual case of a woman student worker who thought of the students part of the time as her children (this is conscious) and part of the time as her sweethearts (this is unconscious).

The image of the woman counselor as a mother figure is reflected in the types of problems brought to women counselors. Vocational problems came first in the survey of female vocational workers' counseling activities. Parents' problems with children came second, children's problems with parents came third, and dating problems came last.

Women counselors seem to have particular difficulty in dealing with sex problems. This has been noted by a number of writers. Snyder says:

It is our feeling that in most instances it is not necessary that the client and counselor be of the same sex. It may at times be a problem, however. An example would be a situation in which a woman counselor would be trying to help a somewhat superstitious and perhaps uneducated man to express his feelings about sexual matters. In such an instance, the man might not be able to overcome his past conditioning to the point of thinking of the counselor as a professional person who could understand and help him.[7]

Speaking to social workers, who would in all probability be women, Garrett similarly says:

Attractive young women interviewers occasionally find it difficult to maintain a professional relationship with a man, especially an adolescent boy or an older man. In their eagerness to be helpful, they sometimes overrespond and, without realizing it, lead the interviewee to believe that they are personally interested in him. Then they are very much embarrassed when asked for a date. They have failed to make clear in their manner the professional nature of the relationship. Had they done so, the interviewee, though attracted, would have gauged the interviewer's interest correctly as a friendly desire to help.[8]

A survey of church people showed that 61 per cent of the men indicated they would not be willing to talk with a woman counselor about a sex problem. Similarly, most of the adolescents indicated that they would be unwilling to discuss a sex problem with a woman. This attitude is borne out by the experience of the professional female religious workers in counseling. Of the total number in this survey only two indicated that their counseling included sex problems. Interestingly enough, these two women were in their forties, seeming to indicate that sex problems are not discussed with younger female counselors.

In the training of women counselors, it may be necessary to emphasize the importance of adequately structuring the situation. Garrett discusses the interest of the male counselee in the female counselor.

When such misinterpretation of the professional nature of the relationship does occur, instead of becoming frightened and withdrawn, the interviewer can best handle the situation by frankly telling the client that she feels she can be of most help if she sees him only during interviews and if they center their discussion primarily about his difficulties. At the same time she should scrutinize her own attitude to make certain that she has not fallen into certain mannerisms that would lead a client to expect too much from her.[9]

For a woman, then, it seems doubly important that she learn to carefully structure the situation. She should make some statement at the beginning of the relationship, pointing out to the counselee the limitations of time and of responsibility and also stressing the point that she is interested in him only as a counselee. It may be necessary for her from time to time, as it is indeed with all counselors, to periodically restructure the situation.

It can be concluded that women have both liabilities and assets in functioning as counselors. On the debit side it seems as if most women are uncertain about assuming the role of counselor, often preferring to see themselves as executives rather than counselors. Because of their emotionality, they may tend to become personally involved in the counseling relationship. They are not always good listeners; they often pay too much attention to detail and, apparently, find it difficult to handle an interview involving the sexual areas of life.

Women have been outstanding in the field of psychiatry, and some vocational experts see psychiatry as a profession for which they are eminently suited. A high executive in the World Council of Churches feels that women are outstanding as counselors in church situations. Their capacity to "bounce back" may help them to empathize more readily. While feminine intuition may cause women to jump at premature conclusions, it would be a great asset in catching the emotional overtones and the nonverbal communications of the counselee.

Woman is the eternal counselor, even though functioning in a completely nonprofessional setting. Husbands, friends, children, neighbors constitute an unending procession of prospective counselees. Her worn kitchen chair may be as effective as the analyst's couch. As she moves into the more formal aspects of counseling, her femininity will enable her to make new and distinctive contributions to the art of counseling.

16. Continuing to Learn

AS IN OTHER arts or skills, there is an unending learning process which must take place if the church leader is to become proficient in his counseling. It was previously noted that there are people who have a natural aptitude for counseling. However, there are not as many as it is sometimes imagined. People very often see themselves as good counselors, but because of lack of knowledge, their counseling sessions easily degenerate into the giving of advice or making other people's decisions. If the maximum efficiency is to be attained, the church leader must continue to learn. It is hoped that the reader of this book will have gained a wider outlook so that he will be stimulated to gain more knowledge of the theory and practice of counseling.

Because the teaching of counseling is relatively new, its techniques are not as yet clearly defined. Approaches to teaching methods in counseling may be grouped around two concepts. In the first, the student makes a study of personality and then goes on to give attention to the various theories upon which counseling techniques are built. The second approach has a resemblance to the old way of teaching a boy to swim by tying a rope around his waist and throwing him into the river. In his struggle to survive, with some advice from a bystander on the bank, he often hit upon some handy ways of keeping himself afloat and sometimes became an effective swimmer. Similarly, after some orientation, the trainee-counselor becomes involved in actual counseling procedures. As he struggles with the counseling situation and is brought face to face with the dynamics of personality, he is compelled to think through his counseling approach, consult his supervisor, and investigate appropriate literature.

Learning the Theoretical Basis of Counseling

It is very easy for people to develop a lofty attitude toward the theoretical basis of any activity, but theory is of vital importance. It has been said that there is nothing so practical as good theory. In counseling, this is particularly so. Most counseling theories can be classified as directive, nondirective, or eclectic.

Directive Counseling

Until fairly recent days, most counseling was thought of in terms of directive theories. In this procedure, the attention of the counselor and the counselee is focused upon a problem and the possibilities for its solution. It is assumed that the counselor is a person of wide experience and knows more than the counselee about the complexities of life. He is able to see through what is being said by the counselee, to understand the problem, and to formulate a plan for the counselee to follow. In keeping with some learning theories, it is concluded that nonneurotic behavior patterns will bring satisfactions and rewards and tend to make the counselee continue in these desirable pathways. It is assumed that the final decisions will be made by the counselee himself, but there is the implication that he will ultimately adopt goals which are considered best by his counselor.

Possibly the clearest formulation of directive counseling is to be found in the writings of Williamson.[1] A modification of his idea follows:

Analysis.—This is the investigatory process by which all information that can be gained is collected from every available source so that the counselor will have a background of material from which to help his counselee.

Synthesis.—All of the information is summarized and organized so that the counselor is able to look over the assets and liabilities of his counselee and evaluate his adjustments and maladjustments.

Diagnosis.—After consideration of all the facts concerned, several conclusions are reached as to the nature and cause or causes of the counselee's problems.

Prognosis.—Having made an evaluation, the counselor then turns his attention to making a prediction as to the possibilities for his counselee. If he decides he cannot help he refers him to someone who can.

Counseling.—During the initial counseling period, it is important that the counselor establish rapport with his counselee. He then proceeds to give the counselee a picture of himself, built from all the information that has been gathered. As the counseling develops, the counselor assists the counselee in making plans for a program of action and then gives his support in translating the plans into action.

Followup.—The counselor continues to help the counselee with his problems or with new difficulties which may arise as the counseling proceeds.

Much of Williamson's book is written from the point of view of a university situation. Nevertheless, there are many aspects which would be relevant to almost any counseling situation. The main criticism of this technique is that it is problem-centered. It was earlier noticed that there is always a possibility that the problem presented may not be the real problem. Like Don Quixote, the counselor may be tilting at a windmill and wasting his time.

The Nondirective Technique

The nondirective technique has been more recently called client-centered therapy. The great personality in the development of this technique is Carl Rogers. His book *Counseling and Psychotherapy,* published in 1942, created tremendous interest in the counseling world.

Many of the fundamental concepts of the nondirective technique are to be found in educational theory. It lays much stress upon the individual's drive toward growth, health, and adjustment. A very important emphasis is that the problems of life are in the emotional rather than the intellectual realm.

Although it is claimed that there is a close link between this theory and psychoanalysis, it does not share the concern about an individual's childhood. Present adjustment is more important than past experiences. It is further claimed that, whereas the directive technique lays a great emphasis upon the problem faced by the individual, here the emphasis is upon the individual rather than upon his problem.

The clearest formulation of the process of the nondirective technique is contained in Rogers' "characteristic steps in therapeutic process." [2] These he sets out as being:

(1) The individual comes for help.

(2) The helping situation is usually defined.

(3) The counselor encourages free expression of feelings in regard to the problem.

(4) The counselor accepts, recognizes, and clarifies these negative feelings.

(5) When the individual's negative feelings have been quite fully expressed, they are followed by the faint and tentative expressions of the positive impulses which make for growth.

(6) The counselor accepts and recognizes the positive feelings which are expressed in the same manner in which he has accepted and recognized the negative feeling.

(7) This insight, this understanding of the self and acceptance of the self, is the next important aspect of the whole process.

(8) Intermingled in this process of insight [there is no rigid order] is a process of clarification of possible decisions, possible courses of action.

(9) Then comes . . . the initiation of minute, but highly significant, positive actions.

(10) There is . . . a development of further insight—more complete and accurate self-understanding as the individual gains courage to see more deeply into his own actions.

(11) There is increasingly integrated positive action on the part of the client.

(12) There is a feeling of decreasing need for help, and a recognition on the part of the client that the relationship must end.

There is often a tendency for people to make the nondirective technique the target of good-natured banter, but the student-counselor should not allow this to cause him to overlook the value of the concept. The nondirective technique has been very influential in the development of pastoral counseling. Clark comments on this:

The counseling technique that has made the greatest impact on religious counselors, with the possible exception of psychoanalysis, is a method which itself owes much to psychoanalysis. This is the so-called "non-directive" or "client-centered" method.[3]

In the emphasis on the value of man, the importance of his growth capacity, and the integrity of his personal decisions, the nondirective technique is truly Christian.

Eclectic Counseling Theory

While there are followers of the several schools of thought who insist on being purists, not deviating from the theories in any way, there are many people who feel that it is possible to take elements of both these systems and make them into a cohesive whole. This approach is generally referred to as eclectic. Some counselors believe that they can alternate between the nondirective and directive methods, using each as the counseling situation demands.

Because the eclectic approach involves the uniting of two apparently contradictory theories, it is not possible to discuss it in any detail. However, Thorne's[4] concepts may be adapted, giving the following guidelines for an eclectic approach:

(1) In general, non-directive methods should be used whenever possible.

(2) Directive methods should be used only when special conditions obtain, and then with caution.

(3) Non-directive techniques should generally be used at the beginning stages of counseling when the counselee is telling his story and also to permit emotional release.

(4) The simplest techniques are the best and the counselor should never become involved in complicated techniques until the simple methods have been tried and found unsuitable.

(5) It is desirable to let the counselee have an opportunity to resolve his problems non-directively. If a counselee is not making progress when non-directive methods are being used, it may be an indication that more directive methods should be utilized.

(6) Directive methods are usually indicated when the counselee is surrounded by circumstances that must be changed or the co-operation of other people sought.

Counseling Courses

Many universities and teachers' colleges offer evening courses in counseling. The emphasis is generally upon guidance, tests, and measurements; but much can be learned which would be applicable to church counseling. This would be particularly so for the church leader who works with young people. Some seminaries and universities offer institutes and courses during the summer months. These may last from one to eight weeks. The American Institute of Family Relations, Hollywood, California, offers an excellent two-week course on marriage counseling techniques. This is generally held in August of each year. There are also centers where courses on counseling are taught in the evenings. The Southern Baptist Seminary Extension Department in Jackson, Mississippi has many of these centers in different parts of the country, and information can be obtained by writing to the director of the Extension Department. There are even some correspondence courses in counseling, but it is doubtful if such courses would be of value; nevertheless, a very fine one has been prepared. Interested readers should contact the American Institute of Family Relations, Hollywood, California.

Books to Help in Counseling

With the developing interest in counseling, there has come a growing body of literature. Many of these books are very well written and easily understood. The church leader who is endeavoring to become a counselor should become as familiar as possible with the present literature in the field.

The following list of books has been graded so that the simpler ones are at the top of the list and the more technical ones near the end. If the beginning counselor reads these, he should acquire knowledge that will help him understand what he is attempting and also give him insight into techniques which he can use.

Pastoral Counseling

BONNELL, J. S. *Psychology for Pastor and People*. New York: Harper & Bros., 1948.

MAY, ROLLO. *The Art of Counseling*. New York: Abingdon Press, 1939.

HULME, WILLIAM E. *How to Start Counseling*. New York: Abingdon Press, 1955.

WISE, CARROLL A. *Pastoral Counseling: Its Theory and Practice*. New York: Harper & Bros., 1951.

DICKS, RUSSELL L. *Pastoral Work and Personal Counseling*. New York: Macmillan Co., 1949.

OATES, WAYNE E. *The Christian Pastor*. Philadelphia: Westminster Press, 1951.

OATES, WAYNE E. (ed.). *An Introduction to Pastoral Counseling*. Nashville: Broadman Press, 1959.

JOHNSON, PAUL E. *Psychology of Pastoral Care*. New York: Abingdon-Cokesbury Press, 1953.

HILTNER, SEWARD. *Pastoral Counseling*. New York: Abingdon-Cokesbury Press, 1949.

Approaches to Personality

WOODWORTH, ROBERT S. *Contemporary Schools of Psychology*. London: Methuen & Co., Ltd., 1951.

JOHNSON, PAUL E. *Personality and Religion*. New York: Abingdon Press, 1957.

OATES, WAYNE E. *The Religious Dimensions of Personality*. New York: Association Press, 1957.

ALLPORT, GORDON W. *Personality: A Psychological Interpretation*. New York: Henry Holt & Co., 1937.

Counseling Theory and Technique

WARTERS, JANE. *Techniques of Counseling*. New York: McGraw-Hill Book Co., Inc., 1954.

ROGERS, CARL R. *Counseling and Psychotherapy*. Boston: Houghton Mifflin Co., 1942.

———. *Client-Centered Therapy*. Boston: Houghton Biffln Co., 1951.

SNYDER, WILLIAM U. *Casebook of Non-Directive Counseling*. Boston: Houghton Mifflin Co., 1947.

Specialized Counseling Areas

GARRETT, ANNETTE. *Interviewing: Its Principles and Methods.* New York: Family Service Association of America, 1942.

YOUNG, RICHARD K. *The Pastor's Hospital Ministry.* Nashville: Broadman Press, 1954.

OATES, WAYNE E. *Where to Go for Help.* Philadelphia: Westminster Press, 1957.

CLINEBELL, HOWARD J., JR. *Understanding and Counseling the Alcoholic.* New York: Abingdon Press, 1956.

KEMP, CHARLES F. *The Pastor and Community Resources.* St. Louis, Missouri: Bethany Press, 1960.

SKIDMORE, REX A., GARRET, HULDA VAN STREETER, and SKIDMORE, C. JAY. *Marriage Consulting.* New York: Harper & Bros., 1956.

WESTBERG, GRANGER. *Premarital Counseling.* New York: National Council of the Churches of Christ, 1958.

JACKSON, EDGAR N. *Understanding Grief.* New York: Abingdon Press, 1957.

HAMRIN, SHIRLEY A. AND PAULSON, BLANCHE B. *Counseling Adolescents.* Chicago: Science Research Associates, Inc., 1950.

Learning from Practical Experiences

Learning the theories is important. Books and other forms of literature are invaluable in the development of counseling skills. But in the final analysis the human document is the important object for our study. A good place to start might be with our own personality and with our peculiar adjustments to life.

Among the psychoanalysts, there is an insistence that the therapist who is learning the art of analysis must himself be psychoanalyzed. There are many who feel that every counselor should have an experience of personal counseling so that he can better understand the counselor-counselee relationship.

If the church leader has a pastor who is interested in counseling or knows of someone who is adequate in this field, it might be advisable for him to have five or six sessions of counseling himself. In an article "How to Be Counseled," Charles F. Kemp suggests:

(1) Begin with the realization that your growth or the satisfactory solution of your problem depends on you.

(2) Recognize the fact that it takes time.

(3) Understand that the solution of your problem depends upon your willingness to persist.

(4) Remember you are the one that must do most of the talking.[5]

A counseling experience entered into with these ideas in mind will probably be very fruitful.

The Clinical Pastoral Education Movement has emphasized the value of the "verbatim report." The verbatim report requires the trainee to visit a patient and write up a detailed report of the conversation which took place.

Seward Hiltner has suggested that this technique might be used in church situations. He calls these "contact reports." When a church leader becomes involved in a problematical situation he takes note of each exchange and later writes it up accurately as he remembers it. He then discusses the incident with some more experienced person. Such a report is not easy but it may enable the church leader to see some of the dynamics involved in the give and take of his counseling techniques.

There is now a considerable amount of material available which may be used by people who are attempting to understand the counseling relationship. One of the distinctive features of Rogers' *Counseling and Psychotherapy*, published in 1942, is a complete verbatim report of a counseling experience. This was the first time such a project had been attempted. Since this time, there have been a number of books which contain material for case study. One of these is Snyder's *A Casebook of Non-Directive Counseling*. It is particularly valuable because in each counseling situation there is one interview annotated so that the counselor's responses and the counselee's statements are categorized. Familiarity with these categories and reading the material will be of great value to the trainee-counselee.

In the appendix of Snyder's book, a portion of a case is presented. The counselor's responses have been removed and a space left so that the student can fill in his own responses. It is then possible for him to turn back to the actual case in the book and see what the trained counselor did in each of these situations and then to make an evaluation of his own responses. This technique of removing the counselor's responses and then endeavoring to respond as if one were the counselor is helpful in developing a sensitivity to the counselee's feelings.

A refinement of the method of reading case studies is that of listening to recordings which have been made of actual counseling experiences. There are not many of these which are freely available, but an excellent record has been prepared by the Pastoral Psychology Book Club. Moreover, there are tapes available from time to time which allow the student to catch something of the emotional overtones of the give-and-take of an interview.

The tape recorder is also of value if it can be used in recording counseling sessions. Care must be taken to see that permission is obtained from the counselee before this is undertaken. As the counselor listens to his own recording he can see more clearly where there is room for improvement in his techniques.

Role-playing offers possibilities in counselor training and only needs two enthusiastic participants. One can take the role of a counselor and the other a counselee. Speaking of such a device Rogers says, "This device may seem artificial, but it develops a surprising amount of reality and at times can become just as real for the counselor as actual therapy." [6] If these role-playing sessions are recorded, the technique becomes of even greater value.

In conclusion, it may be said that in learning counseling, as in any other discipline, the all-important consideration is the motivation of the individual. If a person has a fairly good adjustment to life and believes in the magic of interpersonal relationships, he can learn to counsel effectively. Excellent books are available, many different types of courses are offered by correspondence and in classrooms and within many institutions. If a person really wants to learn to counsel, he can!

17. A Group Counseling Technique

The previous chapters of this book have concentrated on "one-to-one" counseling with no mention of group techniques. This is because there are so many theories of group counseling that an exposition of them would itself be a volume. This chapter centers on just one theory of group counseling, known as "integrity therapy."

The fundamental concepts of integrity therapy can be summed up under the following postulates:

1. Integrity therapy rejects all deterministic theories which make man a victim of heredity, environment, or any other force. Every individual is answerable for himself and exercises his responsibility in making personal decisions.

2. Each person has a conscience, or value system, the violation of which gives rise to guilt. This condition is not a sickness but a result of his wrongdoing and irresponsibility.

3. The typical self-defeating reaction to personal wrongdoing is concealment. In this secrecy, guilt throws up symptoms of varying degrees of severity, from vague discomfort to complete immobilization.

4. As secrecy brought on his trouble and separated him from his fellows, so openness with "significant others" is the individual's first step on the road back to normality.

5. The process of socialization involves a group, which could be called a microcosm or small world, exercising both

a corrective and supportive function for the growing individual.

6. Openness by itself is not enough; the individual is under an obligation to undertake some activity of restitution or penance appropriate to his acknowledged failure in life.

7. The only way to remain a truly authentic person is not only to remain open and make restitution but also to feel a responsibility to carry the "good news" to the people.

Obviously, many ideas in these postulates are similar to widely accepted religious concepts and consequently are applicable to counseling in a church setting. Group counseling opens possibilities for helping more people in a shorter period of time, without many of the disadvantages of the "one-to-one" relationship. It fits easily into church life, where so many of the activities are carried on in groups. The process sets out a series of six steps in an effort to indicate the flow of the counseling procedure.

Step 1: Leading the counselee to see that irresponsibility caused his difficulty.—Few humans, in their honest moments, are really satisfied with themselves and most of us are haunted at some time or another by a sense of failure. The Bible reference to this universal experience says, "There is no difference: for all have sinned, and come short of the glory of God" (Rom. 3:22-23).

The awareness of failure comes from a delicate internal mechanism sometimes referred to as the super ego, or value system, but more generally as conscience. The function of conscience is to indicate to us the relation between our conceived values and our behavior. Its measuring guage is the peculiar human reaction known as guilt, which may throw us into a state of malaise, where we transgress values either consciously or unconsciously held.

In the past, psychologists have had confused attitudes toward conscience. Some have viewed it as a meddlesome and even destructive force. As a result, they have frequently reassured their counselees that there was no need to worry over "such silly little things." This was an effort to allay their clients' fears and to give a measure of comfort.

Now a new wind is blowing in the psychological world. A leading "learning theorist," O. Hobart Mowrer,[1] created a sensation just a few years ago when he insisted that we face the fact that people are "sinners." Of more recent days Psychiatrist Glasser[2] has maintained that many people now described as "sick" are really irresponsible and that excusing their behavior is accomplishing little. Dealing with delinquent girls, he tells a counselee she is not a "shoplifter" but a "thief" and she had better face her irresponsible activity for what it really is.

Here is the beginning point of integrity therapy, which rejects many of the elaborate theorizings. It seeks to transfer the blame for deviant behavior to experiences in the counselee's development. Apart from the traumatic events of his life, what his ancestors were, the type of environment in which he grew, each individual must accept responsibility for himself.

Step 2: Creating an awareness of the self-defeating tendency to ignore and cover up our shortcomings.—Because we live in a society that encourages us to create the best possible image, and because it hurts our pride to acknowledge failure, most of us cannot face "who we are." Instead, we try to gloss over our failures and shortcomings.

One big difficulty in this attitude is that, like the householder who tried to rid himself of an unwanted cat abandoned it on a country road only to be awakened the next morning by a pleading meow at the back door, our transgressions, which we are so sure are hidden, have a strange habit of "coming back home." Symptoms, called by Belgum "the amplified and distorted voice of conscience,"[3] turn up in the most unexpected places. Bodily discomfort, anxiety, depression, irritability, and dreams are only a few of guilt's symptomatic expressions.

Although Shakespeare popularized the expression, "All the world's a stage and men and women merely players," it was Jesus who labeled religious leaders of his day as "hypocrites"— the English translation of a Greek word really meaning "actor." Even the word personality itself comes from a root which means "a mask," implying some type of front put on for our fellows. Few of us need to learn the skills of Hollywood. Our pride helps us to become adept dissemblers, creating an image to the outside world, all the while concealing our past failures.

The tendency of the human ego to be secretive has long been recognized by psychologists who use the words suppression and repression to describe the process whereby the dirty clothes basket of the mind is crammed with soiled experiences we would rather not face. This is true, despite the warning of the Bible, "If we say that we have no sin, we deceive ourselves" (1 John 1:8).

Step 3: Opening a one-to-one dialogue in preparation for group membership.—In this therapy heavy emphasis is laid on the counselor's "modeling" the role he is asking the counselee to play. He wants the anxious counselee to be open with him, and so he becomes open and honest about himself with the counselee.

Mr. Lancaster tells about his restlessness and inability to concentrate on his work. He wonders aloud if he is ever going to be able to regain the vim and vigor which once characterized his life.

The counselor responds, "That's interesting. I recall a personal experience like this. The trouble with me was that I was involved in some dubious behavior. It began to dawn on me that how I *felt* was related to how I *acted*. Is it possible there is 'something' in your life?"

Here is an attempt to enter into dialogue with the troubled person. The counselor is saying, "I, too, am an ordinary human being and known from personal experience that failing to live by conceived values gets us into trouble."

Human nature being what it is, it is remarkable to see how frequently the troubled individual will respond with frankness, candor, and honesty. Historically, Christianity has been a religion in which the followers of Christ have entered into their discipleship because they know that they are sinners. It is surely a strange contradiction that the people who call themselves Christians often experience more difficulty than others in acknowledging their shortcomings. They want to present a good image to the world about them.

Leading the counselee to see his points of failure might well be one of the more subtle parts of the process of integrity therapy. Psychiatrist Glasser, describing his work with delinquent girls, tells of one patient who was a practicing prostitute. She could build up a carefully rationalized justification of her behavior, but when Glasser asked if she wanted her daughter to be a prostitute, her answer was no. Thus, she passed judgment on her own activity.

Step 4: Introducing the counselee to the "small world" or therapeutic group.—Integrity therapy does not remain on a "one-to-one" basis for any length of time. As soon as is practical, the base is widened by introduction to other people with a similar experience and then involvement in the activities of a therapeutic group.

The theory behind the emphasis on the group is that conscience is the "internalized voice of society," and the best way of handling problems of conscience is against the background of a group, whose members become the representatives of an offended society. In this setting the problem can be explored, evaluated, and possible courses of action clarified.

There is no specific size for these groups. They can have as few as three or as many as twelve members. In some instances they are divided by sex, or by age, with special groups for adolescents or other age levels, but the arrangement is flexible and adaptable to particular situations.

In integrity therapy the group performs a twofold function of being supportive and critical. In its supportive aspect it helps to end the isolation and loneliness of emotional upheaval. In one group the common expression is, "We are all fellow strugglers on the sea of life." A group generates a keen interest in its members, leading to concerned inquiries about fellow members.

But this is no mutual interchange of self-pity. The group can become critical and "zero in" on a member who is not accepting responsibility for his actions. Considerable time is sometimes spent evaluating behavior and formulating plans for new efforts to function at a responsible level.

Step 5: Provision of a setting for confessional experiences.— There is no set length of time for a meeting. Sometimes it may be a two-hour period. Some groups start with each member telling of his "hopes and fears," a statement of just what he is looking for or fearing most at the moment. This is done without comment and a member not wishing to participate simply says "pass."

After "hopes and fears," someone is given an opportunity to tell "his story," as the group moves into the confessional step of integrity therapy. Confession is the oldest therapeutic experience known to man and its value is recognized by all systems of psychotherapy. But in integrity therapy there are two distinctives. Confession is never an end in itself; and confession is not made to just one person but to *a group*. The troubled person has offended his conscience, "the internalized voice of society," and the way back is to become at one with the affronted society. The therapeutic group has sometimes been called a "microcosm" or "small world." In this small world the confused person reevaluates himself, his behavior, and his relationships with others. Then he initiates a new process of socialization.

One of the dangers of open confession is that it may be used indiscriminately and become a potential threat to both the confessor and the hearer. Integrity therapy seeks to avoid this by insisting that confession be made only to "significant others." These are either members of the group who by their own honesty have committed themselves to each other or to the persons offended by the deviant activity to be confessed.

Some simple guidelines for confession within groups would be:

(1) We do not confess for others. Other people's lives are their own business, so nothing is repeated outside the group about what is said during the sessions.

(2) Confession is not blaming other people for what happens to us. Whenever a member launches into a recital of what others have done to him, the therapeutic group insists that he focus on his *own* shortcomings, mistakes, and foolishness.

(3) Confession is not complaining. It is all too easy for a counselee to continually complain about his symptom. The group urges him to concentrate more on the way in which he got into his condition.

(4) There is no sense in confessing points of strength. They probably do not need improving. A person seeking healing and strength starts with his own shortcomings. A favorite saying of integrity therapy is, "A man is never stronger than when he is admitting his weaknesses."

The Bible says, "Confess your faults one to another" (James 5:16). When confession takes place in an atmosphere of trust and mutual understanding, it provides a sense of release and an opportunity to discover one's potential. As Jung has said, "It is only with the help of confession that I am able to throw myself into the arms of humanity, freed from the burden of moral exile."[4]

Step 6: Launching out on a venture of purposeful activity.— We have already noted a distinction in integrity therapy procedures, i.e., confession to the group. A second difference is that confession is never an end in itself. Confession must lead to action. Following confession, Mowrer says we "take active steps to change our behavior and rectify past injustices."[5] Consequently, much emphasis is laid on the participant's planning a course of action. The group then helps him to test his plans. If he is to *feel* better he must *act* in a better way.

Sometimes called an action therapy, integrity therapy demands that the client embark on a program of activity in some way related to his irresponsibility. Plans are formulated, reviewed, and checked. As in the Bible, it is constantly insisted that "faith without works is dead."

There is also a missionary aspect of integrity therapy. If a counselee has profited from the experience, he is obligated to tell others. It is expected that when improvement comes the group member will not simply leave the group but continue on in this or some other group to try to help others.

Integrity therapy has been used in many settings—mental hospitals, counseling centers, and community groups—but it is particularly applicable to church situations. However, a church worker should not precipitously launch himself into a career as a group therapist. It would be far more appropriate for the leader to take these principles and quietly apply them as difficult situations present themselves and gradually extend the helping circle. This, in time, could lead to a definite meeting place and give rise to a situation not unlike that referred to by the prophet Malachi, where "they that feared the Lord spake often one to another" (3:16).

Appendix

The Counselor's Loan Shelf

The following books would be valuable additions to a church library.

Courtship

DUVALL, EVELYN MILLIS. *Facts of Life and Love.* New York: Association Press, 1956.

KLEMER, RICHARD H. *A Man for Every Woman.* New York: Macmillan Co., 1959.

MENNINGER, WILLIAM C. *et al. How to Understand the Opposite Sex.* New York: Sterling Publishing Co., Inc., 1956.

Mixed Marriages

PIKE, JAMES A. *If You Marry Outside Your Faith.* New York: Harper & Bros., 1954.

Preparing for Marriage

FISHBEIN, MORRIS, and BURGESS, ERNEST W. *Successful Marriage.* New York: Doubleday & Co., Inc., 1947.

MACE, DAVID R. *Success in Marriage.* New York: Abingdon Press, 1958.

PETERSON, JAMES A. *Education for Marriage.* New York: Charles Scribner's Sons, 1956.

Looking Toward Marriage: a series of Broadman booklets published by the Home Education Department, Sunday School Board of the Southern Baptist Convention:

"There They Go! Will They Be Happy Together?" Claude U. Broach.

"Maturity for Marriage," W. Payton Kolb.

"Looking for Someone?," Ray F. Koonce.

"Marriage and Money," Reuben Herring.

"What Does the Bible Say?," Martha Boone Leavell.

"When Faith Is Not Shared," Vernon B. Richardson.

Sex in Marriage

LEWIN, S. A., and GILMORE, JOHN. *Sex Without Fear.* New York: Medical Research Press, 1950.

STONE, HANNAH, and STONE, ABRAHAM. *A Marriage Manual.* New York: Simon & Schuster, Inc., 1953.

In-Laws

DUVALL, EVELYN MILLIS. *In-Laws: Pro and Con.* New York: Association Press, 1954.

Family Life

ECKERT, RALPH G. *Sex Attitudes in the Home.* New York: Association Press, 1956.

ELLZEY, W. CLARK. *How to Keep Romance in Your Marriage.* New York: Association Press, 1954.

GENNE, WILLIAM H. *Husbands and Pregnancy: Handbook for Expectant Fathers.* New York: Association Press, 1956.

KEMP, CHARLES F. *The Church: The Gifted and the Retarded Child.* St. Louis: Bethany Press, 1958.

LIGON, ERNEST M. *Parent Roles: His and Hers.* Schenectady: Character Research Project, Union College, 1959.

WYNN, JOHN CHARLES. *How Christian Parents Face Family Problems.* Philadelphia: Westminster Press, 1955.

Vocational Choice

BURT, JESSE C. *Your Vocational Adventure.* New York: Abingdon Press, 1959.

FERRARI, ERMA PAUL. *Careers for You.* New York: Abingdon Press, 1954.

KEMP, CHARLES F. *Preparing for the Ministry.* St. Louis: Bethany Press, 1959.

Alcoholism

EARLE, CLIFFORD J. *How to Help An Alcoholic*. Philadelphia: Westminster Press, 1952.

TAYLOR, G. AIKEN. *A Sober Faith: Religion and Alcoholics Anonymous*. New York: Macmillan Co., 1953.

Mental Illness

SOUTHARD, SAMUEL. *The Family and Mental Illness*. Philadelphia: Westminster Press, 1957.

STERN, EDITH. *Mental Illness: A Guide for the Family*. New York: Harper & Bros., 1957.

Notes

Chapter 1

1. Gregor Zilboorg and George W. Henry, *A History of Medical Psychology* (New York: W. W. Norton & Co., Inc., 1941), p. 30.
2. Charles John Ellicott (ed.), *Ellicott's Commentary on the Whole Bible* (Grand Rapids: Zondervan Publishing House, 1954), I, 255.
3. Jacobus, Nourse, Zenos (eds.), *A Standard Bible Dictionary* (New York: Funk & Wagnalls Co., 1909), p. 948.
4. Ellicott, *op. cit.*, VII, 141.

Chapter 2

1. Sheldon Glueck and Eleanor Glueck, "Blueprint for Delinquents," *Time*, LXXIV (Oct. 12, 1959), 62. Used by permission.
2. Viktor E. Frankl, *The Doctor and the Soul* (New York: Alfred A. Knopf, Inc., 1955), p. xix.
3. W. L. Carrington, *Psychology, Religion, and Human Need* (Great Neck, New York: Channel Press, 1957), p. 22.
4. Walter Murdoch, *72 Essays: A Selection* (Sydney: Angus and Robertson, Ltd., 1947), p. 184. Used by permission.
5. Leslie D. Weatherhead, *Psychology, Religion, and Healing* (New York: Abingdon Press, 1951), p. 252. Used by permission.
6. Horace B. English and Ava C. English, *A Comprehensive Dictionary of Psychological and Psychoanalytical Terms* (New York: Longmans, Green & Co., Inc., 1958), p. 533.

Chapter 3

1. John Charles Wynn, *Pastoral Ministry to Families* (Philadelphia: Westminster Press, 1957), pp. 26-27.
2. David R. Mace, "Marriage Guidance in Britain," *Southern Baptist Family Life Education*, V (April, May, June, 1959), 4.
3. Norman Rockwell, "My Adventures As An Illustrator," *Saturday Evening Post* (April 2, 1960), p. 87.

4. Louis P. Thorpe, *The Psychology of Mental Health* (New York: Ronald Press, 1960), p. 89.

5. *Ibid.*, p. 249.

6. Wayne E. Oates (ed.), *An Introduction to Pastoral Counseling* (Nashville: Broadman Press, 1959), p. 287.

Chapter 4

1. Norman R. Jaffray, "Good Listener," *Saturday Evening Post,* CCXXXI (Dec. 6, 1958), 40. Used by permission.

2. H. A. Overstreet, *The Mature Mind* (New York: W. W. Norton & Co., Inc., 1949), pp. 54, 57.

3. *Macbeth,* Act IV, scene 3, lines 208-209.

4. Roland H. Bainton, *Here I Stand: A Life of Martin Luther* (New York: Abingdon Press, 1950), p. 137.

5. Leslie D. Weatherhead, *Prescription for Anxiety* (New York: Abingdon Presss, 1956), pp. 70-76.

6. Ernest R. Groves and Catherine Groves, *Dynamic Mental Hygiene* (Harrisburg: Stackpole and Heck, Inc., 1946), p. 328.

7. Howard J. Clinebell, Jr., *Understanding and Counseling the Alcoholic* (New York: Abingdon Press, 1956), p. 186.

Chapter 5

1. Dominick A. Barbara, *The Art of Listening* (Springfield: Charles C. Thomas, 1958), p. 138. Used by permission.

2. *Second Part of King Henry IV,* Act I, scene 2, lines 136-140.

3. Carl R. Rogers, *Counseling and Psychotherapy* (Boston: Houghton Mifflin Co., 1942), p. 125. Used by permission.

4. Marjorie Holmes, "Why Men Don't Talk to Their Wives," *Today's Health,* published by the American Medical Association, XXXVI (Aug. 1958), 38. Used by permission.

5. Robert T. Oliver, *The Psychology of Persuasive Speech* (2d ed.; New York: Longmans, Green & Co., Inc., 1957), p. 201.

6. Richard W. Wallen, *Clinical Psychology* (New York: McGraw-Hill Book Co., Inc., 1956), p. 364.

7. Arthur Gordon, "The Day at the Beach," *Reader's Digest,* LXXVI (Jan., 1960), 81.

Chapter 6

1. Charles F. Kemp, "The Role of the Religious Counselor in Colleges and Universities" (Doctor's dissertation, University of Nebraska, 1951), p. 81.

2. Arthur H. Brayfield (ed.), *Readings in Modern Methods of*

Counseling (New York: Appleton-Century-Crofts, Inc., 1950), p. 266.

3. Rogers, *op. cit.*, p. 18.

Chapter 7

1. Ordway Tead, *The Art of Leadership* (New York: McGraw-Hill Book Co., Inc., 1935), p. 90.

2. William E. Hulme, *How to Start Counseling* (New York: Abingdon Press, 1955), p. 136.

3. Russell L. Dicks, *Pastoral Work and Personal Counseling* (2d ed.; New York: Macmillan Co., 1949), pp. 125-27.

4. Rex A. Skidmore, Hulda Van Streeter Garret, C. Jay Skidmore, *Marriage Consulting* (New York: Harper & Bros., 1956), p. 111.

5. Rogers, *op. cit.*, p. 31.

6. Clinebell, *op. cit.*, p. 136.

Chapter 8

1. English and English, *op. cit.*, p. 437.

2. Wynn, *op. cit.*, p. 90.

3. Dale Carnegie, *How to Win Friends and Influence People* (New York: Simon & Schuster, Inc., 1936), p. 115.

4. *Ibid.*, p. 125.

5. David Belgum, *Clinical Training for Pastoral Care* (Philadelphia: Westminster Press, 1956), p. 47.

6. Emily H. Mudd, *et al.* (eds.), *Marriage Counseling: A Casebook* (New York: Association Press, 1958), p. 34.

7. Wayne E. Oates, *Where to Go for Help* (Philadelphia: Westminster Press, 1957), pp. 38-40. Used by permission.

8. Emily H. Mudd and Aron Krich (eds.), *Man and Wife* (New York: W. W. Norton & Co., Inc., 1957), p. 210.

9. Wayne E. Oates, *Premarital Pastoral Care and Counseling* (Nashville: Broadman Press, 1958), pp. 45-47.

10. Seward Hiltner, *Pastoral Counseling* (New York: Abingdon-Cokesbury Press, 1949), pp. 82-84.

Chapter 9

1. Charles F. Kemp, *The Pastor and Community Resources* (St. Louis: Bethany Press, 1960), p. 23. Used by permission.

2. Thomas W. Klink, *The Clergyman's Guide to Recognizing Mental Illness* (New York: National Association for Mental Health), pp. 5-8. Used by permission.

3. Oates, *Where to Go for Help*, pp. 32-37.

4. Wayne E. Oates, *The Christian Pastor* (Philadelphia: Westminster Press, 1951), p. 148.

Chapter 10

1. *Macbeth*, Act V, scene 3, lines 40-46.
2. C. E. Erickson, *The Counseling Interview* (New York: Prentice-Hall, Inc., 1950), p. 91.
3. Rollo May, *The Art of Counseling* (New York: Abingdon Press, 1939), p. 173.

Chapter 11

1. Skidmore, Garret, Skidmore, *op. cit.*, p. 284.
2. May, *op. cit.*, p. 151.
3. Harry Stack Sullivan, *The Psychiatric Interview* (New York: W. W. Norton & Co., Inc., 1954), p. 227.
4. Chalmers L. Stacey and Manfred F. Demartino (eds.), *Understanding Human Motivation* (Cleveland: Howard Allen, Inc., 1958), p. 156.
5. Clinebell, *op. cit.*, p. 201.
6. Carroll A. Wise, *Pastoral Counseling: Its Theory and Practice* (New York: Harper & Bros., 1951), pp. 30-31. Used by permission.
7. Reinhold Niebuhr. *The Self and the Dramas of History* (New York: Charles Scribner's Sons, 1955), p. 6.
8. Academy of Religion and Mental Health, *Religion, Science, and Mental Health* (New York: New York University Press, 1959), p. 3.
9. Barbara, *op. cit.*, p. 33.
10. A. A. Brill, *Fundamental Conceptions of Psychoanalysis* (New York: Harcourt, Brace & Co., Inc., 1921), p. 7.
11. Barbara, *op. cit.*, p. 110.
12. Rogers, *op. cit.*, p. 195.
13. Belgum, *op. cit.*, pp. 28-29.
14. Barbara, *op. cit.*, p. 153.
15. Frieda Fromm-Reichmann, *Principles of Intensive Psychotherapy* (Chicago: University of Chicago Press, 1950), p. 7.
16. E. H. Porter, *An Introduction to Therapeutic Counseling* (Boston: Houghton Mifflin Co., 1950), p. 37.

Chapter 12

1. English and English, *op. cit.*, p. 264.
2. Wise, *op. cit.*, p. 137.
3. *Ibid.*, *pp.* 121-34.
4. Gordon W. Allport, *Personality: A Psychological Interpretation* (New York: Henry Holt & Co., 1937), p. 220.
5. *Ibid.*, p. 221.
6. Wise, *op. cit.*, p. 120.

Chapter 13

1. Russell L. Dicks, *When You Call on the Sick* (New York: Harper & Bros., 1938), p. vii.
2. *Ibid.*
3. Wayne E. Oates, "The Inner World of the Patient," *Pastoral Psychology*, VIII (April, 1957), 17.
4. *Ibid.*
5. Dicks, *When You Call on the Sick*, p. vii.
6. Richard K. Young, *The Pastor's Hospital Ministry* (Nashville: Broadman Press, 1954), pp. 55-60.
7. Edgar Jackson, *Understanding Grief* (New York: Abingdon Press, 1957), p. 157.
8. William F. Rogers, "Needs of the Bereaved," *Pastoral Psychology*, I (June, 1950), 19.

Chapter 14

1. Quoted in Skidmore, Garret, Skidmore, *op. cit.*, p. 3.
2. David R. Mace, "Marriage Counseling in Britain Today," *Marriage and Family Living*, XX (Nov., 1958), 379-83.
3. Gerald Gurin, Joseph Veroff, Sheila Feld, *Americans View Their Mental Health* (New York: Basic Books, Inc., 1960), pp. xx-xxi. Used by permission.
4. Wynn, *op. cit.*, p. 26.
5. H. E. Fosdick, *On Being a Real Person* (New York: Harper & Bros., 1943), p. xiv.
6. Mudd, *op. cit.*, p. 52.
7. David R. Mace, *What Is Marriage Counseling* (New York: Public Affairs Committee, Inc., 1957), p. 14.

Chapter 15

1. James Boswell, *Life of Dr. Johnson* (New York: E. P. Dutton & Co., n.d.), I, 266.
2. Russel C. Prohl, *Woman in the Church* (Grand Rapids: Wm. B. Eerdmans Publishing Co., 1957), pp. 77-78.
3. Mary Rebecca Lingerfelter and Harry Dexter Kitson, *Vocations for Girls* (New York: Harcourt, Brace & Co., Inc., 1939), p. 28.
4. Amram Scheinfeld, *Women and Men* (New York: Harcourt, Brace & Co., Inc., 1943), p. 213.
5. Lucius F. Cervantes and Carle C. Zimmerman, *Marriage and the Family* (Chicago: Henry Regnery Co., 1956), as quoted in Paul Popenoe, "Emotional Life of Woman," *Family Life*, XVIII (May, 1958), 2.

6. Eric John Dingwall, *The American Woman: A Historical Study* (New York: Holt, Rinehart and Winston, Inc., 1957), p. 277.

7. William U. Snyder, *A Casebook of Non-Directive Counseling* (Boston: Houghton Mifflin Co., 1947), p. 13.

8. Arnette Garrett, *Interviewing: Its Principles and Methods* (New York: Family Service Association of America, 1942), p. 42. Used by permission.

9. *Ibid.*

Chapter 16

1. E. G. Williamson, *Counseling Adolescents* (New York: Mc-Graw-Hill Book Co., Inc., 1950), pp. 101-26.

2. Rogers, *op. cit.*, pp. 30-44.

3. Walter Houston Clark, *The Psychology of Religion* (New York: Macmillan Co., 1958), p. 15.

4. Frederick C. Thorne, *Principles of Personality Counseling* (New York: McGraw-Hill Book Co., Inc., 1956), pp. 88-89. Used by permission.

5. Charles F. Kemp, "How to Be Counseled," *The Christian*, XCVIII (Jan. 10, 1960), 18. Used by permission.

6. Carl R. Rogers, *Client-Centered Therapy* (Boston: Houghton Mifflin Co., 1951), pp. 468-69.

Chapter 17

1. O. Hobart Mowrer, *The Crisis in Psychiatry and Religion* (Princeton: D. Van Nostrand, 1961), p. 40.

2. William Glasser, *Reality Therapy* (New York: Harper and Row, 1965).

3. David Belgum, *Guilt: Where Psychiatry and Religion Meet* (Englewood Cliffs, N. J.: Prentice-Hall, 1963), p. 49.

4. C. G. Jung, *Modern Man in Search of a Soul* (New York: Harcourt Brace, 1933), p. 35.

5. O. Hobart Mowrer, *The New Group Therapy* (Princeton: D. Van Nostrand, 1964), p. 101.